MAXVORSTADT & SCHWABING

D0421762

Fodor's

Munich's
25Best

by Teresa Fisher

Fodor's Travel Publications
New York • Toronto
London • Sydney • Auckland
www.fodors.com

How to Use
This Book

KEY TO SYMBOLS

✚ Map reference to the accompanying fold-out map

✉ Address

☎ Telephone number

🕐 Opening/closing times

🍴 Restaurant or café

🚆 Nearest rail station

Ⓜ Nearest subway (Metro) station

🚌 Nearest bus route

⛴ Nearest riverboat or ferry stop

♿ Facilities for visitors with disabilities

❓ Other practical information

▷ Further information

ℹ Tourist information

✋ Admission charges: Expensive (over €6), Moderate (€3–€6), and Inexpensive (€3 or less)

★ Major Sight   ★ Minor Sight

👣 Walks   🚌 Excursions

🏬 Shops

🎭 Entertainment and Nightlife

🍴 Restaurants

This guide is divided into four sections

• Essential Munich: An introduction to the city and tips on making the most of your stay.

• Munich by Area: We've broken the city into five areas, and recommended the best sights, shops, entertainment venues, nightlife and restaurants in each one. Suggested walks help you to explore on foot.

• Where to Stay: The best hotels, whether you're looking for luxury, budget or something in between.

• Need to Know: The info you need to make your trip run smoothly, including getting about by public transport, weather tips, emergency phone numbers and useful websites.

Navigation In the Munich by Area chapter, we've given each area its own colour, which is also used on the locator maps throughout the book and the map on the inside front cover.

Maps The fold-out map accompanying this book is a comprehensive street plan of Munich. The grid on this fold-out map is the same as the grid on the locator maps within the book. We've given grid references within the book for each sight and listing.

Contents

ESSENTIAL MUNICH	4–18
Introducing Munich	4–5
A Short Stay in Munich	6–7
Top 25	8–9
Shopping	10–11
Shopping by Theme	12
Munich by Night	13
Eating Out	14
Restaurants by Cuisine	15
If You Like...	16–18

MUNICH BY AREA	19–106
INNENSTADT SÜD	**20–42**
Area Map	22–23
Sights	24–35
Walk	36–37
Shopping	38–39
Entertainment and Nightlife	40
Restaurants	41–42

INNENSTADT NORD	43–58
Area Map	44–45
Sights	46–53
Walk	54
Shopping	55–56
Entertainment and Nightlife	57
Restaurants	58

MAXVORSTADT AND SCHWABING	59–78
Area Map	60–61
Sights	62–72
Walk	73
Shopping	74–75
Entertainment and Nightlife	76
Restaurants	77–78

WEST MUNICH	79–92
Area Map	80–81
Sights	82–88
Walk	89
Shopping	90
Entertainment and Nightlife	91
Restaurants	92

FARTHER AFIELD	93–106
Area Map	94–95
Sights	96–102
Excursions	103–106

WHERE TO STAY	107–112
Introduction	108
Budget Hotels	109
Mid-Range Hotels	110–111
Luxury Hotels	112

NEED TO KNOW	113–125
Planning Ahead	114–115
Getting There	116–117
Getting Around	118–119
Essential Facts	120–121
Language	122–123
Timeline	124–125

Introducing Munich

Think Munich, think beer, BMWs and lederhosen! But there's more to the Bavarian capital than stereotypes. Its unique atmosphere is hard to define but many have tried: 'village of a million'; 'metropolis with a heart'; 'the secret capital of Germany'.

With its big-city atmosphere, rural Alpine charm, art treasures, customs and high-tech industry, this cosmopolitan yet traditional metropolis manages to combine German urban efficiency with Southern European *savoir vivre*. According to a national survey, over half the German population, given the choice, would like to live here. As author Thomas Wolfe once remarked: 'How can one speak of Munich but to say it is a kind of German heaven? Some people sleep and dream they are in paradise, but all over Germany people dream they have gone to Munich.'

The city's close historic associations with the rise of Nazism cannot be ignored. However, we can be grateful that after World War II, although half its buildings were reduced to rubble, unlike so many German cities, Munich chose to restore and reconstruct the great palaces and churches of its past.

Many visitors are attracted to its handsome parks and palaces, its world-class museums, galleries and opera house. Others are drawn by the patriotism and deep-rooted conservatism of its inhabitants who still cherish their age-old folk traditions. For lederhosen and felt hats with shaving-brush tufts are de rigueur here, not to mention the busty dirndl-clad waitresses in the beer cellars clasping at least a dozen steins of lager. And, as you link arms with a stranger to sway to the music of an oom-pah band in one of the city's celebrated beer gardens, the atmosphere brings out the best in everyone: an infectious sociability, a passion for outdoor life and, above all, the Münchners' joie de vivre.

Facts + Figures

- Münchners are the world's largest consumers of beer, downing an annual 190 litres (42 gallons) per head.
- Munich has 25,000 bicycle owners and over 800 sports clubs.
- Munich has Germany's largest university, with over 44,000 students.

MUNICH AND NAZISM

Munich will always be associated with Adolf Hitler. Indeed, he once remarked 'Munich is the city closest to my heart. Here as a young man, as a soldier and as a politician I made my start'. It was here, at the famous bloody Beer Hall Putsch of 1923 when he stormed a meeting of local dignitaries in the Bürgerbräukeller, that he made his first bid for power.

MYSTERY WIND

The famous föhn wind, Munich's unique weather phenomenon, can strike at any time of year. This warm, dry Alpine wind guarantees blue skies and crystal-clear views (the Alps seem close enough to touch) but it is also blamed for headaches and bad moods. So if barmaids seem more short-tempered and the locals blunter than usual, perhaps it's the föhn!

MANN'S SHINING CITY

'München Leuchtet' ('Munich shone'), the opening words of *Gladius Dei* (1902) by the celebrated German writer and Nobel Prize winner Thomas Mann, is without doubt one of Munich's most famous quotations. Today, Munich remains Mann's shining city. His words are on its medal of honour–'Munich shines–on Munich's friends'.

A Short Stay in Munich

DAY 1

Morning Start the day with a traditional Bavarian breakfast of *Weisswürste* (boiled white sausages) at the **Weisses Bräuhaus** (▷ 42). A true Münchner enjoys them with a stein of beer!

Mid-morning Make your way to **Marienplatz** (▷ 29) in the Altstadt (old town). This is where the city's heart beats loudest. The square is dominated by its neo-Gothic town hall. Watch its Glockenspiel in action at 11am or midday, then climb 306 steps up the tower of nearby **Peterskirche** (▷ 31) for a brilliant view of the city.

Lunch Taste some local delicacies from various stands at the **Viktualienmarkt** (▷ 33), known for its vibrant market traders.

Afternoon Head to the **Kunstareal** ('art district') where you can experience a remarkable two millennia of Western art in just a handful of museums and galleries.

Mid-afternoon Choose from the **Staatliche Antikensammlung** or the **Glyptothek** (▷ 67) for classical treasures; the **Alte Pinakothek** (▷ 63) for Old Master paintings; the **Neue Pinakothek** (▷ 69) for medieval to Impressionist art, and the **Pinakothek der Moderne** (▷ 71) for 20th–21st-century collections.

Dinner Return to the heart of the city for a substantial Bavarian meal in **Haxnbauer** (▷ 58), an atmospheric old inn where chefs cook giant shanks of pork *(Schweinshax'n)* over open beechwood fires.

Evening Where better to spend your first evening in Munich than soaking up the atmosphere in the legendary **Hofbräuhaus** (▷ 47)?

Morning All the family will love the world-famous **Deutsches Museum** (▷ 25) with its fascinating hands-on science exhibits.

Mid-morning Shopaholics should enjoy souvenir shopping in the pedestrianized heart of the city. **Kaufingerstrasse** is the main shopping precinct, while **Theatinerstrasse** and **Maximilianstrasse** contain the city's most exclusive boutiques.

Lunch The tiny **Nürnberger Bratwurst Glöckl** (▷ 42) is popular with both locals and tourists alike, with its warm, friendly atmosphere and some of the best sausages in Munich, grilled over an open fire and served with mountains of sauerkraut on pewter plates.

Afternoon Head west to visit **Schloss Nymphenburg** (▷ 85), summer residence of the Wittelsbachs, and to stroll in its magnificent grounds; or relax in the **Englischer Garten** (▷ 65), Munich's famous 'green lung', where locals go walking, jogging, busking, swimming and sunbathing.

Mid-afternoon Enjoy some refreshment at the **Chinesischer Turm** (▷ 65) beer garden, one of Germany's largest beer gardens, seating 7,000 people.

Dinner Tuck into some traditional Bavarian fare at **Spatenhaus** (▷ 58), before crossing Max-Weber-Platz for an evening's operatic entertainment at the celebrated **Nationaltheater** (▷ 48, 57). If opera is not your style, there's sophisticated **Schumann's** (▷ 57) for cocktails.

Evening Party animals will find plenty of late-night bars and clubs in the **Gärtnerplatz** district, or head to trendy **Schwabing** to see and be seen.

Top 25

▶▶▶

Alte Pinakothek ▷ **62–63** One of the most important galleries in the world for Old Master paintings.

Viktualienmarkt ▷ **33** Bavaria's largest and best-known open-air food market.

Spielzeugmuseum ▷ **32** This antique toy collection is a must for children, with its teddy bears and train sets.

Schloss Nymphenburg ▷ **84–85** One of Germany's largest baroque palaces and its grand park.

Schleissheim ▷ **100** Don't miss the masterpieces in the Great Gallery of the Neues Schloss.

Residenz ▷ **50–51** It is easy to imagine the Wittelsbachs' glorious heyday in the state rooms of this impressive palace.

Pinakothek der Moderne ▷ **70–71** One of the world's largest museums devoted to the visual arts.

Asamkirche ▷ **26** A masterpiece of rococo architecture in the midst of a busy shopping street.

Bavaria Filmstadt ▷ **96–97** Glimpse behind the scenes of Europe's largest film studios.

Peterskirche ▷ **31** Munich's beloved ancient parish church has sweeping bird's-eye views.

Olympiapark ▷ **82–83** Scene of the 1972 Olympic Games, this extensive park is hugely popular.

Odeonsplatz ▷ **49** This city square is flanked by historic buildings and steeped in history and tradition.

These pages are a quick guide to the Top 25, which are described in more detail later. Here they are listed alphabetically, and the tinted background shows which area they are in.

Bayerisches National-museum ▷ **46** A taste of Bavarian life over the centuries.

BMW Museum ▷ **86** This dazzling museum provides a fascinating display of transport technology.

Dachau ▷ **98–99** A pretty town that is also the site of the first Nazi concentration camp.

Deutsches Museum ▷ **24–25** One of the largest and best science museums in the world.

Englischer Garten ▷ **64–65** Popular for walking, cycling, sunbathing or relaxing in a beer garden.

Frauenkirche ▷ **27** The twin onion-shape domes are a symbol of Munich.

Hofbräuhaus ▷ **47** The world's most famous pub, a munich institution.

Königsplatz ▷ **66–67** The Glyptothek, the Antikensammlung and the Propyläen reside here at 'Athens-on-the-Isar'.

Lenbachhaus ▷ **68** A delightful gallery of 19th- and 20th-century art housed in a Italianate villa.

Marienplatz ▷ **28–29** The city's main square, and a great place to people-watch.

Neue Pinakothek ▷ **69** The 19th- and 20th-century art and sculpture are a must for aficionados.

Nationaltheater ▷ **48** Restored to its pre-war glory and home to the Bavarian State Opera.

Münchner Stadtmuseum ▷ **30** The city's vibrant history from medieval times to the present day.

Shopping

Munich's most popular shopping street is without doubt the pedestrian zone between Karlsplatz and Marienplatz—one kilometre (half a mile) of shopping fun with huge department stores interspersed with boutiques and supermarkets. Even when the shops are closed this area is packed with window-shoppers. German fashions, leather and sportswear are all good buys. Just off Marienplatz, sports fans will revel in the giant sports department stores of Schuster and SportScheck (▷ 39), where you can buy everything from golf tees to skiing holidays.

Munich Fashion

Munich is the capital of Germany's fashion industry, and you will be amazed at the city's range of boutiques from haute couture and Bavarian *Trachten* (folk costume) to wacky new trends. In the elegant shops of Theatinerstrasse, Residenzstrasse and Maximilianstrasse famous designer labels rub shoulders with the classic Munich boutique of Bogner (▷ 55). Be sure to visit Loden-Frey (▷ 56), the largest shop for national costume in the world—look for articles in Loden cloth, a Bavarian specialty. This waterproof wool fabric in grey, navy or traditional green, has kept Münchners warm in winter for generations.

CULINARY DELIGHTS

Local culinary specialties include countless types of sausage, best eaten with *Süßsenf* (sweet mustard), as well as fine regional herbs, breads and cheese, all magnificently displayed on green wooden stalls at the traditional open-air Viktualienmarkt (▷ 33), while Dallmayr (▷ 55) and Feinkost Käfer (▷ 56) are among the finest delicatessens in Europe. For truly unique chocolates, visit Elly Seidl (▷ 55), famous for its *Münchner Küppeln* chocolates, shaped like the onion-domes of the Frauenkirche.

Tulips on Neuhauserstrasse (top left); a nutcracker stall at the Christmas Market (middle)

Publishing and Porcelain

As one of the world's leading publishing cities, with over 3,000 publishing houses, it is hardly surprising that Munich boasts a wide variety of bookshops, concentrated in the city's core and near the university in Schellingstrasse. Antiques shops, too, are popular, with many specialising in 'English', Jugendstil (art nouveau) and art deco styles. Collectors keep a look out for old Meissen or modern Rosenthal, while the famous Nymphenburg porcelain (▷ 56, 90)—produced in Munich since 1747—is still manufactured in its traditional rococo designs. For the finest in Bavarian handicrafts, visit the Kunstgewerbeverein (▷ 56) in Pacellistrasse, or the numerous streets converging on Max-Joseph-Platz, for unique Bavarian gifts, including handmade puppets, carnival masks and porcelain beer steins.

Beer and Breweries

No shopping spree would be complete without purchasing some of Munich's beer. The main breweries are Spaten-Franziskaner, Augustiner, Löwenbräu, Hacker-Pschorr, Hofbräuhaus and Paulaner. There are special glasses for special beers, special beers for certain seasons. And with beer halls everywhere, it won't take long to find out if you prefer *dunkles*, *Weissbier*, *Pils* or *helles*… As they say in Munich, *Prost!*

Shopping in Maximiliansplatz (top right); Munich's open-air Viktualienmarkt (above)

SPECIALTY SHOPPING

Munich has a large number of small, old-fashioned shops that concentrate on one or two articles—for example, musical boxes, felt, buttons, knives, wood-carvings and even lederhosen—and which are still to be found in the middle of town. Some of the best buys in Munich include German-made binoculars, telescopes, kitchenware, electronic gadgets and bed linen. The presence of so many top orchestras in Germany results in top-notch musical instruments. Germany is also known for its manufacture of children's toys. You'll find everything from train sets and teddybears to traditional dolls and handmade puppets.

Shopping by Theme

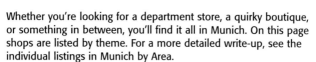

Whether you're looking for a department store, a quirky boutique, or something in between, you'll find it all in Munich. On this page shops are listed by theme. For a more detailed write-up, see the individual listings in Munich by Area.

ANTIQUES

Antike Uhren Eder (▷ 55)
Hugendubel (▷ 38)
Landpartie (▷ 74)

BOOKS

Deutsches Museum Shop
    (▷ 38)
Words' Worth (▷ 74)

CHILDREN

Kinder-Ambiente (▷ 74)
Kunst und Spiel (▷ 74)
Obletter (▷ 39)
Die Puppenstube (▷ 74)

DEPARTMENT STORES

Galeria Kaufhof (▷ 38)
Karstadt (▷ 38, 90)
Ludwig Beck (▷ 39)
Olympia
    Einkaufszentrum (OEZ)
    (▷ 90)
SportScheck (▷ 39)

FASHION

Behringer (▷ 55)
Bogner (▷ 55)
Bree (▷ 55)
Eduard Meier (▷ 55)
Flip (▷ 74)
Fourth Dimension (▷ 38)
Hallhuber (▷ 74)
Hemmerle (▷ 56)
Hirmer (▷ 38)

Konen (▷ 38)
Lederhosen Wagner
    (▷ 39)
Loden-Frey (▷ 56)
Move Sportshoes (▷ 90)
Theresa (▷ 56)

FOOD AND MARKETS

L'Antipasto (▷ 90)
Armin's Räucherkuchl
    (▷ 90)
Boettner (▷ 55)
Le Chalet du Fromage
    (▷ 74)
Dallmayr (▷ 55)
Eilles (▷ 55, 90)
Elisabethmarkt (▷ 74)
Elly Seidl (▷ 55)
Espresso & Barista (▷ 90)
Feinkost Käfer (▷ 56)
Markt am Wiener Platz
    (▷ 56)
Rischart (▷ 39)
Schmidt (▷ 39)
Spanisches Fruchthaus
    (▷ 39)
Viktualienmarkt (▷ 33, 39)

GIFTS AND BAVARIAN SOUVENIRS

Butlers (▷ 55)
Geschenke Kaiser (▷ 38)
Holz Leute (▷ 39)
Kunstgewerbeverein (▷ 56)
Max Krug (▷ 39)
Porzellanmanufaktur
    Nymphenburg
    (▷ 56, 90)
Stockhammer (▷ 74)

Weihnachtsmarkt
    (▷ panel 39, 90)

INTERIOR DESIGN AND ART

2-Rad (▷ 74)
Deco Susanne Klein
    (▷ 38)
Hussfeld Zang (▷ 90)
Kaut-Bullinger (▷ 38)
Kokon (▷ 56)
Kremer Pigmente (▷ 74)
Kristina Sack (▷ 90)
Schreibmayr (▷ 56)

SPECIALIST SHOPS

China's World (▷ 74)
Dehner (▷ 38)
Derstet Sinne (▷ 55)
Fanshop (▷ 55)
Grödner Holzschnitzereien
    (▷ 90)
Messer & Scheren (▷ 39)
Perlenmarkt (▷ 74)
Rosenthal Studio-Haus
    (▷ 56)

Munich by Night

Munich's nightlife is relatively small-scale and provincial compared to some cities. On a mild summer's evening, nothing beats strolling through the old town, seeing the illuminated historic buildings, or pausing to enjoy a drink or an ice cream on the broad sidewalk terraces of Leopoldstrasse.

Eating and Drinking

Eating and drinking in Munich are major pastimes, with options ranging from hearty Bavarian fare washed down with massive litre-steins of beer in the local Bierkellers to some of Germany's finest restaurants. In both beer cellars and beer gardens, it is normal to sit together with other guests at long communal tables.

City of Music

Munich is a city of music, with a famous opera-house long associated with Mozart, Wagner and Richard Strauss, and three major symphony orchestras. The *Münchner Festspiele* festival in July and August marks the musical highpoint of the year, attracting top international singers and opera aficionados. There's always something musical happening, from choral works and organ recitals in churches, open-air concerts in royal palaces, to live jazz, blues and rock venues, not to mention marionette-opera performances and even yodelling. If your German is good enough, Munich also offers a dazzling schedule of first-rate theatre, ranging from classical and contemporary productions to political cabaret.

Fun and beer-drinking at the Oktoberfest (top and middle); Cuvilliés-Theater in the Residenz (above)

NIGHT SPOTS

Early-closing laws prevent many places from staying open all night, but Munich has plenty of vibrant bars and clubs, many on Gärtnerplatz, the student district of Schwabing and the Glockenbach quarter. Choose from foaming beer steins and drunken swaying to the oom-pah bands of the beer halls or sophisticated cocktails in Germany's trendiest nightspots.

Eating Out

Bavarian food, usually accompanied by a beer, is hearty and heavy and is almost always based on meat. White sausages, dumplings, sauerkraut and roast pork are just a few examples of local cuisine. Beer halls *(Brauhäuser)* are the best places to try traditional German food and sample some of the city's own beers.

Italian Connection
Munich has a strong affinity with Italy, which means the city has plenty of Italian restaurants. Locals share the Italians' love of dining alfresco —at the first hint of sunshine, chairs and tables are swiftly moved outside to terraces, court-yards and gardens. In recent years, the number of Thai, Japanese, Mexican and tapas restaurants in the city has also grown.

When to Eat
In Munich, people like to eat early and it is not unusual to find older Munich residents having lunch as early as 11.15am. As hotel breakfast buffets are substantial, you may not be hungry enough for an early lunch. In this case, choose one of the many bars, cafés and restaurants that serve full meals or even breakfast right into the afternoon. In the evening, those restaurants that aren't open all day start serving at about 6pm. Non-smokers will likely be pleased to learn that smoking is banned in bars, cafés and restaurants except in separate rooms (where these exist).

BÄCKEREIEN AND *KAFFEE UND KUCHEN*

Bakeries *(Bäckereien)* are usually the first eateries to open in the morning. They serve an overwhelming array of cakes, pastries, breads and coffees at very reasonable prices. Many bakeries have a small seating or standing area, so you can eat your purchases there. Cafés in Germany also often open as early as 7 or 8am, and tend to serve a wide range of light snacks, in addition to *Kaffee und Kuchen* (coffee and cakes), which are usually enjoyed mid-morning or late in the afternoon.

Café Glockenspiel; a Munich beer garden; a street café in Neumarkt; traditional Würste

Restaurants by Cuisine

There are restaurants to suit all tastes and budgets in Munich. On this page they are listed by cuisine. For a more detailed description of each restaurant, see Munich by Area.

AFTERNOON TEA

Kempinski Hotel Vier
  Jahreszeiten (▷ 58)
Schlosscafé im
  Palmenhaus (▷ 92)

BAVARIAN CUISINE

Augustiner
  Gaststätten (▷ 41)
Bachmaier Hofbräu (▷ 77)
Hacker-Pschorr Bräuhaus
  (▷ 92)
Halali (▷ 58)
Haxnbauer im
  Scholastikahaus (▷ 58)
Hofbräuhaus (▷ 47)
Hundskugel (▷ 41)
Löwenbräukeller (▷ 92)
Nürnberger Bratwurst
  Glöckl (▷ 42)
Ratskeller (▷ 42)
Schlemmermeyer (▷ 42)
Spatenhaus an der Oper
  (▷ 58)
Weisses Bräuhaus (▷ 42)
Zum Alten Markt (▷ 42)

BEER GARDENS

Augustiner-Keller (▷ 92)
Hirschgarten (▷ 92)
Kloster Andechs (▷ 102)
Max Emanuel Bräuerei
  (▷ 77)
Seehaus im Englischen
  Garten (▷ 78)
Taxisgarten (▷ 92)

Waldwirtschaft
  Grosshesselohe
  (▷ 102)
Zum Flaucher (▷ 102)
Zur Schwaige (▷ 92)

CAFÉS

Café Altschwabing (▷ 77)
Café Frischhut (▷ 41)
Café Glockenspiel (▷ 41)
Café Haidhausen (▷ 41)
Café Puck (▷ 77)
Café Schwabing (▷ 77)
Café Wiener Platz (▷ 58)
Dukatz im
  Literaturhaus (▷ 58)
Eisbach (▷ 58)
Kostbar (▷ 92)
News Bar (▷ 77)
Tresznjewski (▷ 78)

GOURMET

Bogenhauser Hof (▷ 58)
Käfer-Schänke (▷ 58)
Königshof (▷ 41)
Lenbach (▷ 77)
Rue des Halles (▷ 42)
Tantris (▷ 78)
Terrine (▷ 78)

ICE CREAM

Adamello (▷ 41)
Sarcletti (▷ 92)

INTERNATIONAL CUISINE

Le Cézanne (▷ 77)
Grissini (▷ 77)
Joe Peña's (▷ 41)
Maredo (▷ 41)
Osteria (▷ 78)
Papatakis (▷ 78)
Rosso Pizza (▷ 78)
Sausalito's (▷ 78)
Seoul (▷ 78)
La Stella (▷ 78)
Tiramisu (▷ 78)
Trader Vic's (▷ 58)
Vinaiolo (▷ 42)

SNACKS

Münchner Suppenküche
  (▷ 42)
Nordsee (▷ 42)
Vincenz Murr (▷ 42)
Vini e Panini (▷ 78)

VEGETARIAN

Buxs (▷ 41)
Café Ignaz (▷ 77)
Café Ruffini (▷ 92)
Prinz Myshkin (▷ 42)

If You Like...

However you'd like to spend your time in Munich, these top suggestions should help you tailor your ideal visit. Each sight or listing has a fuller write-up elsewhere in the book.

EXPLORING ON A SHOE-STRING

Visit Munich's churches for free, including lofty Frauenkirche (▷ 27), sumptuous Asamkirche (▷ 26) and beautiful Theatinerkirche (▷ 49).
Window-shop on glamorous Maximilianstrasse, with its glitzy designer boutiques.
Climb the Olympiaturm (▷ 82–83) for spectacular views of the city and its Alpine backdrop.
While away an afternoon people-watching in the Englischer Garten (▷ 64-65).

CHILDREN'S ACTIVITIES

Star in a movie at the Bavaria Filmstadt (▷ 96–97).
Enjoy a dazzling performance at Munich's internationally acclaimed Circus Krone (▷ 91).
Marvel at science at the Deutsches Museum (▷ 24–25).
Visit the world's first 'Geo-Zoo' (▷ 102).

The Olympic Tower; the 4-D Cinema Experience at the Filmstadt (above)

STAYING IN LUXURY

Check into Munich's top hotel, the Kempinski Vier Jahreszeiten (▷ 112).
Be pampered at Le Meridien's luxurious spa (▷ 112).
Enjoy the top-notch restaurant at the majestic Königshof hotel (▷ 112).
Cosset yourself in the stylish surroundings of boutique hotel Ritzi (▷ 112).

LOCAL DELICACIES

Order the best *Weisswürste* in town at the Weisses Bräuhaus (▷ 42).
Try some *Leberkäs* (meat loaf), or *Bratwurst* with sweet mustard, from one of the stands at the Viktualienmarkt (▷ 33).
Tuck into a gigantic pork shank (*Schweinshax'n*) at Haxnbauer (▷ 58).

Spa pampering (above right); a traditional meal of beer and sausages (right)

An evening of jazz; enjoying a stein of beer (below)

LIVE MUSIC

Chill out at the city's celebrated Jazzclub Unterfahrt (▷ 57).

Enjoy an evening of yodelling at the tiny Jodlerwirt (▷ 57)—there's nothing more Bavarian.

Assess the future of German classical music at a concert or recital in the Hochschule für musik (▷ 72).

DRINKING BEER

Try the Bavarian beer at the legendary Hofbräuhaus (▷ 47).

See and be seen at Hirschgarten beer garden (▷ 92).

Relax at the Chinesischer Turm beer garden in the Englischer Garten (▷ 64–65).

Enjoy live jazz at the atmospheric Grosshesselohe beer garden (▷ 102).

CONTEMPORARY ARCHITECTURE

Tour the new, space-age Allianz Arena football stadium (▷ 101).

Notice how BMW's towering HQ (▷ 87) resembles a four-leaf clover.

See a symbol of modern Munich: Olympiapark's futuristic tent-roof (▷ 82).

Visit the 21st-century Herz-Jesu-Kirche (▷ 87), which boasts the world's largest church doors.

Herz-Jesu-Kirche (above)

SHOPPING FOR BAVARIAN SOUVENIRS

Try on some *Trachten* (Bavarian folk costume) at Loden-Frey (▷ 56).

Taste glühwein and gingerbread while shopping at the annual *Weihnachtsmarkt* on Marienplatz (▷ panel, 39).

Shop for the fine pewter ornaments that make unusual and attractive gifts at Geschenke Kaiser (▷ 38).

The Weihnachtsmarkt *(Christmas Market, left)*

BIRD'S-EYE CITY VIEWS

Frauenkirche; freshly squeezed juices (below)

Dine in the revolving restaurant atop the Olympiaturm (▷ 82–83), with its breathtaking views of the city and the Alps.
Climb the steps of Peterskirche's tower (▷ 31) for the best bird's-eye views of the city.
Look down on Marienplatz from the Neues Rathaus (▷ 28–29) viewing tower.
Climb one of the celebrated onion domes atop the Frauenkirche (▷ 27) for 360-degree views of the city.

EATING BRUNCH

Join the beautiful people for eggs Benedict and freshly squeezed juices at Eisbach (▷ 58).
Head to Kostbar (▷ 92) for delicious all-day breakfasts.
Try trendy Café Schwabing for a traditional Bavarian brunch (▷ 77).

HIP BARS

Rub shoulders with models and celebrities at Schumann's (▷ 57), Munich's most sophisticated bar.
Take your pick at sleek P1 (▷ 57), which offers Munich's beautiful people a choice of eight bars to suit all tastes and moods.
Mix with the stylish Gärtnerplatz crowd at Interview (▷ 40).
Enjoy exotic cocktails at Master's Home (▷ 40), a long-standing favourite with Münchners.

Cocktails (above); Peterskirche and the maypole (below)

BEAUTIFUL CHURCHES

Marvel at the lavish interior and religious treasures of the Asamkirche (▷ 26).
Admire the lofty Michaelskirche (▷ 35), the largest Renaissance church north of the Alps.
Hear the bells chime at Peterskirche (▷ 31), the city's oldest parish church.
Seek out the Devil's footprint inside Munich's Frauenkirche cathedral (▷ 27).

Munich by Area

Sights	24–35
Walk	36–37
Shopping	38–39
Entertainment and Nightlife	40
Restaurants	41–42

INNENSTADT SÜD

Sights	46–53
Walk	54
Shopping	55–56
Entertainment and Nightlife	57
Restaurants	58

INNENSTADT NORD

Sights	62–72
Walk	73
Shopping	74–75
Entertainment and Nightlife	76
Restaurants	77–78

MAXVORSTADT AND SCHWABING

Sights	82–88
Walk	89
Shopping	90
Entertainment and Nightlife	91
Restaurants	92

WEST MUNICH

| Sights | 96–102 |
| Excursions | 103–106 |

FARTHER AFIELD

The city centre is where Munich's heart beats loudest. From Marienplatz, the main square, it's just a stone's throw to the city's cathedral, the robust daily market and the main pedestrian shopping precinct.

Sights	24–35	Top 25	**TOP 25**
Walk	36–37	Deutsches Museum ▷ 24	
		Asamkirche ▷ 26	
Shopping	38–39	Frauenkirche ▷ 27	
		Marienplatz ▷ 28	
Entertainment		Münchner Stadtmuseum	
and Nightlife	40	▷ 30	
		Peterskirche ▷ 31	
Restaurants	41–42	Spielzeugmuseum ▷ 32	
		Viktualienmarkt ▷ 33	

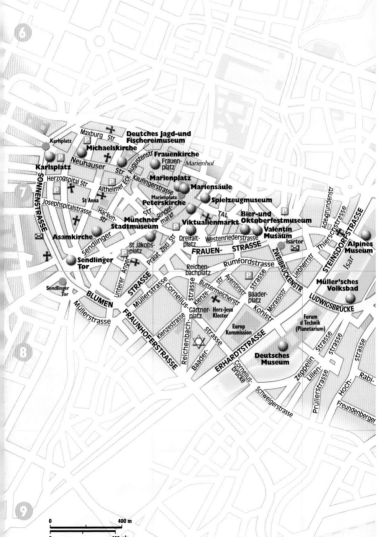

Karlsplatz

Karlsplatz

Maxburg Str

Deutches Jagd-und
Fischereimuseum

Michaelskirche

Neuhauser Str

Augustenstr

Frauenkirche

Frauen-
platz

Marienhof

Herzogspital Str

Altheimer Eck

Kaufingerstrasse

Marienplatz

Mariensäule

St Anna

Hacken str

Sendlinger Str

Burgstr

Peterskirche

Marienplatz

Spielzeugmuseum

Josephspitalstrasse

SONNENSTRASSE

Münchner
Stadtmuseum

Viktualienmarkt

TAL

Bier-und
Oktoberfestmuseum

Asamkirche

Sendlinger Str

St Jakobs-
platz

Prät Zist Str

Dreifalt-
platz

Westenriederstrasse

Valentin
Musäum

Isartor

STEINSDORFSTRASSE

Adelgrundenstr

Thierschstrasse

Alpines
Museum

Sendlinger
Tor

Sendlinger
Tor

Unterer Anger

FRAUEN-
STRASSE

Reichen-
bachplatz

Rumfordstrasse

Liebherrstr

Isar

ZWEIBRÜCKENSTR

Müller'sches
Volksbad

BLUMEN
STRASSE

Müllerstrasse

FRAUNHOFERSTRASSE

Müllerstrasse

Cornelius
strasse

Klenzestrasse

Reichenbach

Buttermelcherstr

Klenze str

Aventinstr

Baader-
platz

Kohlstr

Morassistr

LUDWIGSBRÜCKE

Forum
d Technik
(Planetarium)

Gärtner-
platz

Herz-Jesu
Kloster

Baader

Europ
Kommission

ERHARDTSTRASSE

Cornelius
strasse

Deutsches
Museum

Cornelius-
brücke

Schweigerstrasse

Zeppelin
strasse

Lilien-
strasse

Prüllerstrasse

Hoch-
strasse

Rabl-
strasse

Freudenberger

0 ——— 400 m

0 ——— 400 yds

H · J · K

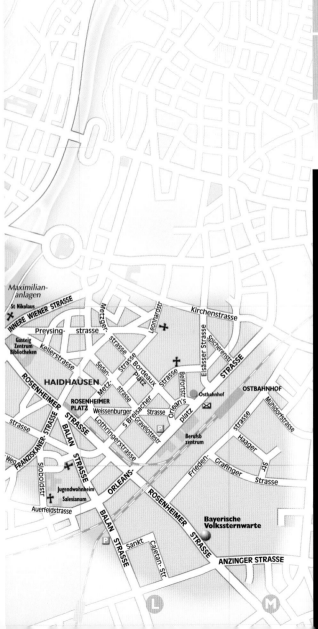

Maximilian-
anlagen
St Nikolaus
INNERE WIENER STRASSE
Kirchenstrasse
Preysing-   strasse
Metzger-
strasse
Leonhardtstr
Elsässer Strasse
Söcheinstr
Gasteig
Zentrum
Bibliotheken
Kellerstrasse
STRASSE
Sedan-
strasse
strasse
Bordeaux
Platz
strasse
Belfortstr
ROSENHEIMER STRASSE
HAIDHAUSEN
Metz-
strasse
Ostbahnhof
OSTBAHNHOF
ROSENHEIMER
PLATZ
Weissenburger   Strasse
Orlean's
platz
Mühldorfstrasse
strasse
S Breisacher
GravelotteStr
strasse
Lothringerstrasse
Berufsb
zentrum
Haager
P
Frieden-
grafinger
str
Strasse
FRANZISKANER- STRASSE
BALAN
STRASSE
Weg
Sloboldstr
Jugendwohnheim
Salesianum
ORLEANS-
ROSENHEIMER
Auerfeldstrasse
Bayerische
Volkssternwarte
BALAN
STRASSE
P
STRASSE
Sankt
Cajetan- str
ANZINGER STRASSE

Deutsches Museum

HIGHLIGHTS

- Planetarium
- Karl Benz's Automobil Nummer I
- Copy of the 'Puffing Billy' steam train
- Reconstruction of a coal mine
- Dornier Do 31 and Junkers Ju 52 aircraft
- 19th-century sailing ship— 60m (197ft) long

TIP

- The museum shop is a great source for science books, souvenirs and quality museum-endorsed gifts to appeal to all ages (tel: 21 79 224).

If you spent one minute at each exhibit, it would take you 36 days to see everything at this museum of superlatives— Munich's most famous and Germany's most visited science museum.

Voyage of discovery In 1903, engineer Oskar von Miller founded the Museum of Masterworks of Science and Technology. After his death, the collection moved to its present building on its own island on the Isar, east of the city and was officially opened in 1925. Over the years this giant technological 'playground' has grown to a staggering 17,000-plus exhibits, ranging from the sundial to the space shuttle.

Learning experience The most popular areas cover mining (including a reconstructed coal

The Deutsches Museum sits on its own island on the Isar and houses one of the world's greatest collections of scientific and technological exhibits

mine), computer science and various transportation sections. Alongside original objects are audio-visual displays, experiments and hands-on models.

Unique exhibits Some of the most dramatic displays are the star shows at the Planetarium (which take place in the high-tech Forum), an ear-splitting high-voltage demonstration that simulates a 220,000-volt flash of lightning, and the vast model railway on the ground level. Other highlights are a reconstruction of the caves at Lascaux; the first German U-boat (submarine); one of the first jet planes; Karl Benz's first car; a massive train track featuring many types of train; and the bench on which Otto Hahn proved the splitting of the atom. The exhibits constantly evolve to reflect the latest historical and technological discoveries.

THE BASICS

www.deutschesmuseum.de

✚ J8

✉ Museumsinsel 1

☎ 2179-1

🕐 Daily 9–5

🍴 Restaurant, café

🚇 S-Bahn Isartor; U-Bahn Fraunhoferstrasse

🚌 131; tram 8

♿ Excellent

💶 Moderate

Asamkirche

TOP 25

The church of St. John Nepomuk is known as Asamkirche after its architects

THE BASICS

🔒 H7

✉ Sendlinger Strasse 62

☎ 260 9171

🕐 Mon–Fri 7.30–6, Sat 8–7, Sun 8–3

🚇 U-Bahn Sendlinger Tor

🚌 152; tram 17, 18, 27

♿ Free

❓ Free tours (in German) Thu at 4pm

HIGHLIGHTS

● *Gnadenstuhl (Throne of Mercy)*, E. Q. Asam
● Ceiling fresco, C. D. Asam
● Two-tiered high altar
● Wax effigy of St. John Nepomuk
● Statues of John the Baptist and St. John the Evangelist
● Portraits of the Asam brothers
● Façade

The Asamkirche may be Munich's finest rococo structure. A narrow but sensational façade provides a mere hint of the sumptuous interior—one of the most lavish works of the celebrated Asam brothers.

The Asam brothers In 1729, master architect and sculptor Egid Quirin Asam acquired a house in Sendlinger Strasse and built his own private church next door, assisted by his brother, a distinguished fresco artist. For this reason, the Church of St. John Nepomuk (a Bohemian saint popular in 18th-century Bavaria) is better known as the Asamkirche. Even though Asam financed the construction, he was forced to open it to the public, and the church was consecrated in 1746. Free from the normal constraints of a patron's demands, the brothers created a dazzling jewel of rococo architecture.

Lavish decoration The unobtrusive marble façade has an unusual plinth of unhewn rocks and a kneeling figure of St. John Nepomuk. The tiny, dark but opulent interior is crammed with sculptures, murals and gold leaf, and crowned by a magnificent ceiling fresco depicting the life of the saint. The long, narrow nave carries your eye straight to the glorious two-tiered high altar and shrine of St. John Nepomuk. The gleaming gallery altar, portraying the Trinity and illuminated by an oval window representing the sun, is crowned by Egid Quirin's *Throne of Mercy*, depicting Christ crucified, in the arms of God, wearing the papal crown.

The twin towers of Frauenkirche are the symbol of Munich

Frauenkirche

This massive, late-Gothic brick church symbolizes Munich more than any other building. Its sturdy twin towers (99m/325ft and 100m/328ft high), with their Italian-Renaissance onion domes, dominate the city's skyline.

Munich's cathedral The Frauenkirche, built between 1468 and 1488, has been the cathedral of Southern Bavaria since 1821. Today's structure, the largest reconstructed medieval building in Munich, has been rebuilt from the rubble of World War II. Little remains of the original design except the basic architectural elements and the windows in the choir. Its strength lies in its simplicity and grand proportions.

Onion domes Thirty years after the church's consecration, the towers were still roofless. In 1524, unique green Italian-Renaissance onion domes were erected as a temporary measure. With this eccentric addition to the structure, the building once provoked an irreverent comparison to a pair of beer mugs with lids. However, the domes became so popular that they were retained.

The Devil's footprint A footprint is visible in the stone floor by the entrance. Legend has it that the Devil visited the church and stamped his foot in delight because the architect had apparently forgotten to put in windows, though the building was flooded with light. But Jörg von Halsbach's ingenious design meant that no windows were visible from this point, thus giving him the last laugh.

THE BASICS

✚ J7
✉ Frauenplatz 1
☎ 290 0820
🕐 Sat–Thu 7–7, Fri 7–6
🚇 U- or S-Bahn Marienplatz
🚌 52, 131, 152; tram 19
♿ None
🎫 Free

HIGHLIGHTS

● Gothic stained-glass windows
● The Baptism of Christ, Friedrich Pacher altarpiece
● Jan Polack altar panels
● St. Lantpert's Chapel with wood figures of apostles and prophets from the workshop of Erasmus Grasser

TOP 25

Marienplatz

HIGHLIGHTS

● Glockenspiel
● Façade
● Tower
● Ratskeller (▷ 42)

TIP

● Don't miss Konrad Knoll's famous Fish Fountain here, on the site of a former fish market. They say if you wash your purse here on Ash Wednesday, it will never be empty. The Lord Mayor still washes the City Purse here every year.

Eleven o'clock is the magic hour for tourists who crowd Marienplatz to see the world-famous Munich Glockenspiel in action on the lavish neo-Gothic façade of the New Town Hall.

Towers and turrets Marienplatz is the city's main square, and traditionally the scene of tournaments, festivals and ceremonies. It is also a great place to people-watch. The entire north side of the square is dominated by the imposing Neues Rathaus (New Town Hall), seat of the city government for nearly a century. Constructed between 1867 and 1909 around six courtyards with towers and turrets, sculptures and gargoyles, its neo-Gothic style was controversial at the time, but the Neues Rathaus has since become one of Munich's best-known landmarks.

Marienplatz, with the famous Glockenspiel on the Neues Rathaus (New Town Hall), is the heart of the city

The Glockenspiel On the main front of the building, figures of Bavarian royalty stand alongside saints and characters from local folklore. The central tower viewing platform offers a fantastic view of the city, and houses one of the largest Glockenspiels (carillons) in Europe. This mechanical clock plays four different tunes on 43 bells while 32 almost life-size carved figures present scenes from Munich's history—among them the jousting match at the marriage of Duke Wilhelm V with Renate of Lorraine in 1568, and the *Schäfflertanz* (Coopers' dance) of 1517, celebrating the end of the Black Death. This dance is re-enacted in Munich's streets every seven years (next in 2011). Both Glockenspiel events can be seen daily at 11am and also at noon and at 5pm in summer. The cuckoo that ends the performance always raises a smile.

THE BASICS

✚ J7

✉ Marienplatz

☎ 23 300 (Neues Rathaus)

🕐 Tower: Nov–Apr Mon–Fri 10–5, May–Oct 10–7

🍴 Ratskeller beer hall and restaurant

🚇 U- or S-Bahn Marienplatz

🚌 52, 131, 152

♿ Few

💷 Tower: inexpensive

Münchner Stadtmuseum

The City Museum is housed in the former armoury

THE BASICS

www.stadtmuseum-online.de
+ H7
✉ St.-Jakobs-Platz 1
☎ 233 22370
🕐 Tue–Sun 10–6
🍴 Café and beer garden
Ⓤ U-Bahn Sendlinger Tor, U- or S-Bahn Marienplatz
🚌 52, 131 152
♿ Good
💰 Moderate
❓ Tours, lectures

HIGHLIGHTS

● History of the City section
● Marionette Theatre Collection and fairground museum
● Photography and Film Museum

INNENSTADT SÜD TOP 25

Munich's unique, lively, eclectic personality is reflected in the diverse nature of the City Museum's collections, which range from weapons, armour and fashion to fairgrounds, Biedermeier and films.

City history If your itinerary does not allow enough time to explore all the old parts of the city on foot, head straight to the History of the City section housed on the first floor, to study Munich's development since the Middle Ages through maps, models and before-and-after-photographs, which illustrate the devastating effects of World War II bombing.

Unusual collections As the museum is housed in the former city armoury, it is only fitting that it should contain one of the largest collections of ancient weaponry in Germany. Other collections worth visiting include fashion from the 18th century to the present day, the second-largest musical instrument collection in Europe and the Photography and Film Museum, with its fascinating display of ancient cameras and photographs. Don't miss the greatest treasure—Erasmus Grasser's 10 *Moriske* Dancers (1480), magnificent examples of late Gothic secular art, originally carved for the Old Town Hall (▷ 32).

For children of all ages On the third floor the Marionette Theatre Collection (Münchner Marionettentheater), one of the world's largest, reflects Bavaria's role in the production of glove-puppets, shadow plays and mechanical toys.

*The tower of
Peterskirche with its
lantern-dome*

Peterskirche

THE BASICS

- J7
- Petersplatz
- 260 4828
- Tower Mon–Sat 9–6, Sun 10–6 (until 7 in summer). Closed in bad weather
- U- or S-Bahn Marienplatz
- 52, 131, 152
- None
- Tower: inexpensive

Known affectionately to Münchners as 'Alter Peter', the city's oldest parish church is immortalized in a traditional song that claims 'Until Old Peter's tower falls down, we'll have a good life in Munich town'.

Built over time The Peterskirche dates from the foundations of the city itself in 1158, on a slight hill called the Petersbergl, where the monks (who gave their name to Munich) had established a settlement in the 11th century. The original Romanesque structure was expanded in Gothic style and renovated.

Destruction and rebirth During World War II the church was almost entirely destroyed. In an attempt to raise money to rebuild it, Bavarian Radio stirred the hearts of the people of Munich by playing only a shortened version of the 'Alter Peter' song, and public donations flowed in. After the tower was completed, in October 1951, the full version was at last heard again.

Bells and a view The most extraordinary feature is the tower with its lantern-dome and eight asymmetrically placed clock-faces, designed so that, according to Karl Valentin (▷ 35), eight people can tell the time at once. The chimes are renowned and include one of the largest bells in Germany: The best time to hear them is at 3pm on Saturday, when they ring in the Sabbath. The 306-step climb to the viewing platform is rewarded by a dramatic bird's-eye view of Munich.

HIGHLIGHTS

- High Altar (Nikolaus Stuber, Egid Quirin Asam and Erasmus Grasser)
- Clock tower
- Schrenk Altar
- Jan Polack's five Gothic pictures
- Mariahilf Altar (Ignaz Günther)
- Corpus-Christi Altar (Ignaz Günther)
- Aresinger-Epitaph (Erasmus Grasser)

Spielzeugmuseum

The enchanting Toy Museum in the Gothic tower of the Altes Rathaus

THE BASICS

www.spielzeugmuseum-muenchen.de

✚ J7

✉ Altes Rathausturm, Marienplatz

☎ 294001

🕐 Daily 10–5.30

🚇 U- or S-Bahn Marienplatz

🚌 52, 131, 152

♿ None

💷 Moderate

HIGHLIGHTS

● Steiff teddy bears
● Hauser-Elastolin collection
● Smallest doll in the world
● Jumping jacks from Oberammergau
● Moscovian painted puppets
● Model Zeppelin
● First ever Bakelite toy television

With its turrets, towers and romantic Gothic façade, Munich's Old Town Hall provides a fairy-tale setting for this nostalgic collection of antique toys. It is one of the city's most popular children's attractions.

Toys galore It's easy to miss the tiny entrance to the Toy Museum, hidden at the foot of the grand Gothic tower of the Altes Rathaus' (Old Town Hall) on the southeast corner of Marienplatz. From here, a narrow spiral staircase leads up to four floors of neatly arranged European and American toys dating from the last two centuries.

Old and new Start with the teddy bears, toy soldiers, dolls and model cars belonging to local caricaturist Ivan Steiger at the top. Then work your way down, tracing the history of toys, starting with old dolls, animals and folk toys dating back to 1780, from Bohemia, Vienna, Russia and other famous European toymaking areas. Don't miss the folk toys from Berchtesgaden, the world's smallest doll and the celebrated Steiff teddy bears.

Dolls and carousels Lower down the tower, a splendid collection of carousels and steam engines is followed by part of the Hauser-Elastolin archive collection, named after one of Germany's main toy producers, and a series of American toys including Felix the Cat and Humpty Dumpty, and other childhood delights. Look out also for the sophisticated model train layouts, and the fine collection of dolls and dolls' houses.

The Viktualienmarkt in spring and in winter

Viktualienmarkt

Less than a stone's throw from the cosmopolitan shops of Munich's main pedestrian zone, this bustling open-air food market, with taverns and cooked food stands, has retained its traditional atmosphere for centuries.

A long tradition In 1807 it was decided that the market in Marienplatz had become too small for the rapidly growing trade. So a new Viktualienmarkt was planned for a grassy field outside the city, where livestock grazed and stagecoaches stopped. Today it is Munich's oldest, largest and most attractive market with its quaint green wooden stalls and jazzy striped umbrellas.

Atmosphere The lively atmosphere of the market owes much to the robust market women, famous for the loud and lively abuse they dish out in earthy Bavarian dialect to their customers. Their goods are superb, the prices high and the variety of fresh produce is vast, ranging from Bavarian blue cheese to Alpine herbs and flowers. Look out for neatly tied bundles of asparagus in spring, and mountains of fresh cranberries in summer.

Open-air restaurant Try some Bavarian specialties from the little taverns and stands dotted around the market—*Leberkäs* (meat loaf) or a *Brat-* or *Weisswurst* (fried or white sausage)—wash it down with a typically Bavarian *Weissbier* (a light beer made using top-fermentation yeast) in the beer garden set up round the maypole, the scene of lively May Day celebrations.

THE BASICS

www.viktualienmarkt-muenchen.de

➕ J7

🕐 Mon–Fri 7.30–6, Sat 7.30–1

🍴 Numerous stands serve hot and cold snacks

Ⓜ U- or S-Bahn Marienplatz

🚌 52, 131, 152

HIGHLIGHTS

● Irene Schwarz—more than 40 different kinds of potato
● Exoten Müller—freshly pressed fruit juices
● Rottler—herbs, mustards, preserves and chutneys
● Münchner Suppenküche—soup kitchen (▷ 42)
● Nordsee—fish snacks (▷ 42)
● Pferdemetzgerei Wörle—specialty horsemeat sausages
● Ludwig Freisinger—herbs and spices
● Honighäusl—herbal honey wines

More to See

ALPINES MUSEUM

www.alpenverein.de

Everything you want to know about mountaineering in the Alps from 1760 onwards, plus occasional temporary exhibitions.

➕ K7 ✉ Praterinsel 5 ☎ 211 2240 🕐 Tue–Fri 1–6, Sat, Sun 11–6 🚇 U- or S-Bahn Isartor 🚃 Tram 17 💵 Moderate

BAYERISCHE VOLKSSTERNWARTE

www.sternwarte-muenchen.de

The Bavarian Observatory is fascinating, and a special late-night treat for children. Friendly staff will help you find specific stars and comets, and there's a planetarium as well.

➕ L9 ✉ Rosenheimer Strasse 145 ☎ 40 62 39 🕐 Sep–Mar Mon–Fri 8pm–10pm; Apr–Aug Mon–Fri 9pm–11pm 🚇 U-Bahn Karl-Preis-Platz 💵 Moderate

BIER- UND OKTOBERFEST-MUSEUM

www.bier-und-oktoberfestmuseum.de

With its six breweries Munich is undoubtedly the world's number one beer metropolis. This special museum is devoted to beer and its most famous celebration, the *Oktoberfest*. Learn about the history of beer and discover why Munich's beer is so special.

➕ J7 ✉ Sterneckerstrasse 2 ☎ 2423 1607 🕐 Tue–Sat 1–5 🚇 S-Bahn Isartor 💵 Moderate

DEUTSCHES JAGD- UND FISCHEREIMUSEUM

www.jagd-fischerei-museum.de

The German Hunting and Fishing Museum has the most important collection of its kind in Germany, including the Wolpertinger, a 'hoax' animal resembling a marmot with webbed feet, antlers and wings.

➕ H7 ✉ Neuhauserstrasse 2 ☎ 22 05 22 🕐 Daily 9.30–5 (Thu until 9) 🚇 U- or S-Bahn Marienplatz 💵 Moderate

MARIENSÄULE

Marienplatz owes its name to this gracious figure of the Virgin Mary. All distances in Bavaria are measured from this point.

A boar guards the entrance to the Hunting and Fishing Museum

The Mariensäule and the Neues Rathaus

🚉 J7 ✉ Marienplatz 🚇 U- or S-Bahn
Marienplatz

MICHAELSKIRCHE

www.st-michael-muenchen.de
The largest Renaissance church
north of the Alps, the Jesuit
Church of St. Michael was built at
the end of the 16th century by Duke
Wilhelm (the Pious) as a monument
to the Counter-Reformation. Disaster
struck in 1590 when the tower
collapsed; it was finally consecrated
in 1597. War damage has been
masterfully repaired, Marvel at the
Renaissance hall with its ornate, barrel-
vaulted roof.
🚉 H7 ✉ Neuhauserstrasse 52
☎ 231 7060 🕐 Mon–Sat 10–7 (Thu
until 8.45), Sun 6.50am–10.15pm 🚇 U- or
S-Bahn Karlsplatz 🚋 Tram 16, 17, 18, 19, 20,
21, 27 💶 Free

MÜLLER'SCHES VOLKSBAD

Germany's loveliest indoor swimming
pool, in the Jugendstil style.
🚉 K8 ✉ Rosenheimer Strasse 1 ☎ 79 62
23 🚇 S-Bahn Isartor 🚋 Tram 18

SENDLINGER TOR

The medieval Sendlinger Tor town
gatehas a large central arch and two
hexagonal flanking towers. It was once
the southern exit of the town walls.
🚉 H7 🚇 Sendlinger Tor

VALENTIN-MUSÄUM

www.valentin-musaeum.de
Showcase for the eccentric
humour of Munich's Karl Valentin
(1882–1948), Bavaria's answer to
Charlie Chaplin, much-loved for his
quirky wit and misanthropic humour.
He started out in beer halls but soon
attracted the attention of Schwabing
intellectuals and is perhaps best
remembered for his sketch in which
he put fish in a bird-cage and birds in
an aquarium. The museum contains
various oddities, and has bizarre
opening times too.
🚉 J7 ✉ Tal 50 ☎ 223266 🕐 Mon, Tue,
11.01–5.29; Fri, Sat 11.01–5.59; Sun
10.01–5.29 🚇 S-Bahn Isartor 💶 Free

Müller'sches Volksbad–a Jugendstil public bath

Munich's Old Town

Explore the pedestrian heart of Munich, between its medieval west and east gates, with its cathedral, main square and market.

DISTANCE: 2km (1.2 miles) **ALLOW:** 2 hours (excluding visits)

START ┄┄┄┄

KARLSPLATZ
✚ H7 Ⓢ S- and U-Bahn Karlsplatz

❶ Pass through Karlstor, site of the former medieval west gate to the city, into Neuhauserstrasse, the main pedestrian shopping zone. Don't miss the Michaelskirche (▷ 35) on the left.

❷ Turn left on Augustenstrasse to Frauenkirche (▷ 27), the cathedral, with its distinctive onion-shape domes. Return to the main shopping area via Liebfrauenstrasse and on to Marienplatz (▷ 28–29).

❸ Head up Rindermarkt (beside Hugendubel bookshop, ▷ 38) to the Peterskirche (▷ 31). If you're feeling energetic, climb the tower—the view of the city is worth the effort.

❹ Swing round the side of the church to the Viktualienmarkt (▷ 33), for some light refreshment in the beer garden or from one of the small food stands there.

┄┄┄┄ **END**

KARLSPLATZ
✚ H7 Ⓢ S- and U-Bahn Karlsplatz

❽ Head back along Tal towards Marienplatz. Just before you enter the square, visit the Toy Museum (▷ 32), in the Old Town Hall. Cross Marienplatz, continue up Neuhauserstrasse back to the startpoint.

❼ Turn right into Westenrieder Strasse then first left up Sterneckerstrasse past the Bier- und-Oktoberfestmuseum (▷ 34). Continue on to Tal. Turn right toward Isartor, Munich's most easterly remaining medieval gate. Inside one tower is the museum devoted to Karl Valentin (▷ 35).

❻ You will come to Gärtnerplatz, site of the celebrated Staatstheater (▷ 40). Proceed past the bars and restaurants of Klenzestrasse, cross Rumfordstrasse and Frauen Strasse until you reach Zwinger Strasse.

❺ Cross to the far side of the market and continue down Reichenbachstrasse.

Shopping

DECO SUSANNE KLEIN

A tiny boutique near Gärtnerplatz, specializing in modern furniture, plush fabrics and state-of-the-art interior design.

🚇 J8 ✉ Klenzestrasse 41 ☎ 272 2427 🚇 U-Bahn Fraunhoferstrasse 🚌 52, 152

DEHNER

www.dehner.de
Full of great gift ideas for garden lovers. What about a packet of Alpine flower seeds or even a grow-your-own 'Bavarian meadow'?

🚇 J7 ✉ Frauen Strasse 8 ☎ 2423 9980 🚇 S-Bahn Isartor

DEUTSCHES MUSEUM SHOP

www.deutsches-museum-shop.com
An amazing, eccentric shop full of books, toys, puzzles and models based on the scientific and technical world, for children and adults.

🚇 J8 ✉ Museumsinsel 1 ☎ 2138 3892 🚇 S-Bahn Isartor 🚋 Tram 18

FOURTH DIMENSION

www.fourthdimension.de
One of Germany's leading costume jewellery shops. Smart but affordable.

🚇 J7 ✉ Frauenplatz 14 ☎ 2280 1090 🚇 S-Bahn Marienplatz

GALERIA KAUFHOF

www.galeria-kaufhof.de
One of several Kaufhof department stores here; centrally located.

🚇 J7 ✉ Kaufingerstrasse 1–5 ☎ 23 18 51 🚇 U- or S-Bahn Marienplatz

GESCHENKE KAISER

www.geschenke-kaiser.de
Pewter Christmas decorations, serving dishes, candlesticks and beer jugs are the specialties here.

🚇 J7 ✉ Rindermarkt 1 ☎ 26 45 09 🚇 U- or S-Bahn Marienplatz

HIRMER

www.hirmer-grosse-groessen.de
A first-class clothing shop with six floors exclusively for men.

🚇 H7 ✉ Kaufingerstrasse 28 ☎ 23 68 30 🚇 U- or S-Bahn Marienplatz

HOLZ LEUTE

www.holz-leute.de
Everything here is made of wood, with decorative and functional items

BARGAIN-HUNTING

Munich has over 8,000 shops and 15 big department stores and there are plenty of bargains to be had if you know where to look. Start with the department stores that sell cut-price goods in their basements, and always keep your eyes open for *Sonderangebot* (special offer) signs. The best bargains can be found at the end-of-season sales in January and July.

ranging from games to biscuit cutters.

🚇 J7 ✉ Viktualienmarkt 2 ☎ 26 82 48 🚇 U- or S-Bahn Marienplatz

HUGENDUBEL

www.hugendubel.de
A giant branch of the book 'supermarket' chain, spread over four floors. There are even sofas where you can sit and read to your heart's content without buying! There are several more branches in the city.

🚇 J7 ✉ Marienplatz 22 ☎ 01801 48 44 84 🚇 U- or S-Bahn Marienplatz

KARSTADT

www.karstadt.de
This giant department store has six outlets in the city, this one, Haus Oberpollinger am Dom, sells electical appliances, books, furnishings, cosmetics and clothing.

🚇 H7 ✉ Neuhauserstrasse 18 ☎ 29 02 30 🚇 U- or S-Bahn Karlsplatz

KAUT-BULLINGER

www.kaut-bullinger.de
Three floors of chic stationery ranging from pens, writing paper and art materials to leather personal organizers and designer wrapping paper.

🚇 J7 ✉ Rosenstrasse 8 ☎ 23 80 00 🚇 U-or S-Bahn Marienplatz

KONEN

www.konen.de
A reliable fashion shop full of leading inter-

national labels for women, men and children.

➕ H7 ✉ Sendlinger Strasse 3 ☎ 244 4220 🚇 U-Bahn Sendlinger Tor

LEDERHOSEN WAGNER

This shop has been making Bavaria's distinctive leather shorts from soft deerskin since 1825. Surprise your friends with a 'shaving brush' hat, made out of chamois hair, to match the shorts.

➕ J7 ✉ Tal 2 ☎ 22 56 97 🚇 U- or S-Bahn Marienplatz

LUDWIG BECK

www.ludwigbeck.com
Beck is without doubt Munich's most stylish department store. At Christmas artisans work on the top floor and the store becomes a winter wonderland of handicrafts.

➕ J7 ✉ Marienplatz 11 ☎ 23 69 10 🚇 U- or S-Bahn Marienplatz

MAX KRUG

www.max-krug.com
Old Bavaria lives in this trove of traditional souvenirs and knick-knacks—handmade wooden cuckoo clocks, beer steins and more.

➕ H7 ✉ Neuhauserstrasse 2 ☎ 22 45 01 🚇 U- or S-Bahn Karlsplatz

MESSER & SCHEREN

A specialist knife and scissor shop—excellent for left-handers too.

➕ K8 ✉ Rosenheimer Strasse 42 ☎ 480 1392 🚇 S-Bahn Rosenheimer Platz

OBLETTER

www.obletter.de
Comprehensive toy shop selling everything from cuddly toys to train sets. Other branches.

➕ H7 ✉ Karlsplatz 11–12 ☎ 5508 9510 🚇 U- or S-Bahn Karlsplatz

RISCHART

www.rischart.de
One of many Rischart shops offers the largest choice of bread, rolls and cakes in town.

➕ J7 ✉ Marienplatz 18 ☎ 231 7000 🚇 U- or S-Bahn Marienplatz

SCHMIDT

Shop here for some of the best *Lebkuchen*

WEIHNACHTSMARKT

Every Advent, Marienplatz comes alive with the magic of Christmas, with one of Germany's finest Christmas markets, and the air is filled with the aroma of Glühwein and roasted chestnuts. A spectacular 30m (100ft) Christmas tree is erected in the middle of the square, and surrounded by tiny wooden huts selling traditional crafts, toys, candles and Christmas decorations: look out for festive Nutcracker dolls, hand-carved crib sets and *Lebkuchen* (gingerbread) hearts.

(delicious gingerbread), which are presented in collectable tins, along with *Stollen* (traditional festive fruitcakes).

➕ J7 ✉ Westenriederstrasse 6 ☎ 2323 8980 🚇 S-Bahn Isartor

SPANISCHES FRUCHTHAUS

A mouth-watering display of dried fruits entices you into this small shop with an unusual selection of crystallized, fresh and chocolate-coated fruits.

➕ J7 ✉ Rindermarkt 10 ☎ 26 45 70 🚇 U- or S-Bahn Marienplatz

SPORTSCHECK

The department store for sports fanatics. Six floors are dedicated to every sport imaginable. It's just an hour by car to the nearest ski slopes, and the store will even arrange day-long ski trips to the mountains.

➕ H7 ✉ Sendlinger Strasse 6 ☎ 21660 🚇 U-Bahn Sendlinger Tor

VIKTUALIENMARKT

www.viktualienmarkt-muenchen.de
The largest and most famous Bavarian open-air food market. Look out for the Kräuter- stand Freisinger stand for herbs and the Honighäusl stand for honey products.

➕ J7 🕐 Mon–Fri 7.30–6, Sat 7.30–1 🚇 U- or S-Bahn Marienplatz

Entertainment and Nightlife

CAFÉ GLOCKENSPIEL
www.cafe-glockenspiel.de
Opposite Marienplatz's
famous Glockenspiel
(▷ 28–29), the roof-
terrace cocktail bar and
1970s-style Expresso
bar-café here are
always crowded.
➕ J7 ✉ Marienplatz 28
(5th floor) ☎ 26 42 56
🕐 10am–1am 🚇 U- or
S-Bahn Marienplatz

GASTEIG
www.gasteig.de
Home of the Munich
Philharmonic Orchestra
and the city's main
cultural hub.
➕ K8 ✉ Rosenheimer-
strasse 5 ☎ 48 09 80
🚇 S-Bahn Rosenheimer Platz

HAVANNA CLUB
www.havannaclub-
muenchen.de
Ernest Hemingway
images are among the
'stars' of this dark, intimate bar decorated in
Spanish colonial style.
➕ J7 ✉ Herrnstrasse 30
☎ 29 18 84 🕐 Mon–Wed
6pm–1am, Thu–Sat 6pm–2am,
Sun 7pm–1am 🚇 S-Bahn
Isartor

ICE RINK
Skate under the stars on
this outdoor ice rink.
Skate rental is available,
and the rink is surround-
ed by stands selling
snacks such as steaming
glühwein.
➕ H7 ✉ Karlsplatz 🕐 Late
Nov–end Jan daily 10.30–10
🚇 U- or S-Bahn Marienplatz

MASTER'S HOME
www.mastershome-
muenchen.de
An extraordinary under-
ground bar in the
colonial style of a typical
African farmhouse. Sit in
the bathroom, the
bedroom, the living room
or at the bar, which is
cooled by a giant
aeroplane propeller,
and eat, dance or simply
lap up the atmosphere
over a delicious cocktail.
➕ J7 ✉ Frauenstrasse 11
☎ 22 99 09 🕐 Daily
6pm–2am 🚇 S-Bahn Isartor

MORIZZ
www.club-morizz.de
This plush bar draws a
cool, and often gay
clientele, for cocktails
and sophisticated snacks.
➕ J8 ✉ Klenzestrasse 43
☎ 201 6776 🕐 7pm–2am
(Fri–Sat till 3am) 🚇 U-Bahn
Fraunhoferstrasse 🚌 152

MÜNCHNER FILMMUSEUM
www.stadtmuseum-
online.de/filmmu.htm
Screenings (Tuesday–

ALL-NIGHT PARTYING
Compared with some cities,
Munich's nightlife is small-
scale and provincial. Due to
early-closing laws, most bars
close around 1am and most
nightclubs at 4am. However,
the Backstage Club, nick-
named 'House of the Rising
Sun', with its techno and
house music sometimes
doesn't even open until 6am.

Sunday) from Germany's
largest collection of
silent movies.
➕ H7 ✉ St.-Jakobs-Platz 1
☎ 2332 4150 🚇 U-Bahn
Sendlinger Tor,
U- or S-Marienplatz

MUSEUM LICHTSPIELE
www.movietown.eu
This former music hall
frequently shows English-
language films.
➕ K8 ✉ Lilienstrasse 2
☎ 0180 5867 0777 🚇 S-
Bahn Rosenheimer Platz
🚊 Tram 27

ODODO
A simple, stylish bar,
appealing to a diverse
clientele, for its unusual
mix of fondues and
exotic cocktails.
➕ J8 ✉ Buttermelcher-
strasse 6 ☎ 260 7741
🕐 Mon–Thu 11am–1am,
Fri 11am–3am, Sat 6pm–3am,
Sun 6pm–1am 🚇 U-Bahn
Fraunhoferstrasse
🚊 Tram 17, 18

STAATSTHEATER AM GÄRTNERPLATZ
www.staatstheater-am-
gaertnerplatz.de
This flourishing theatre
claims to be the only
municipal light
opera-house in the
world, with a wide
repertoire of operetta,
light opera, musicals and
ballet.
➕ J8 ✉ Gärtnerplatz 3
☎ 02411 🚇 U-Bahn
Fraunhoferstrasse 🚌 52, 56

Restaurants

INNENSTADT SÜD

RESTAURANTS

PRICES

Prices are approximate, based on a 3-course meal for one person.
€€€ over €50
€€ €25–€50
€ under €25

ADAMELLO (€)

Hidden in a quiet backstreet in Haidhausen, this Italian-run café sells the best ice cream in town. The specialty—*Coppa Adamello*—containing a mountain liqueur, is delicious.
✚ L8 ✉ Preysingstrasse 29 ☎ 48 32 83 🕐 Daily 11–6 (midnight in summer) 🚊 Tram 18

AUGUSTINER GASTSTÄTTEN (€€)

www.augustiner-restaurant.com
Munich's oldest still-standing brewery, now a popular inn, serves reasonably priced Bavarian fare. Beer was brewed here until 1897.
✚ H7 ✉ Neuhauserstrasse 27 ☎ 2318 3257 🚇 U- or S-Bahn Karlsplatz

BUXS (€)

www.buxs.de
You pay by the weight of your plate in this cafeteria-style vegetarian restaurant, which serves an impressive array of hot and cold dishes.
✚ J7 ✉ Frauenstrasse 9 ☎ 291 9550 🕐 Mon–Fri 11–6.45, Sat 11–3 🚇 S-Bahn Isartor

CAFÉ FRISCHHUT (€)

Early birds meet night owls for strong coffee and delicious deep-fried *Schmalznudeln* doughnuts as early as 5 in the morning.
✚ J7 ✉ Prälat-Zistl-Strasse 8 ☎ 26 82 37 🕐 Mon–Fri 7–6, Sat 5–5 🚇 U- or S-Bahn Marienplatz

CAFÉ GLOCKENSPIEL (€€€)

www.cafe-glockenspiel.de
One of Munich's most romantic settings directly opposite the Glockenspiel. There's also a popular café and bar (▷ 40).
✚ J7 ✉ Marienplatz 28 ☎ 26 42 56 🕐 Restaurant daily 10–11.30. Café daily 10–1 🚇 U- or S-Bahn Marienplatz

CAFÉ HAIDHAUSEN (€)

Look out for the 'Hangover' breakfast or

RUSTIC ATMOSPHERE

Wooden tables covered with blue-and-white check tablecloths, benches and carved chairs lend a warm feel to a typical Bavarian restaurant. Murals depicting mountains, lakes and hunting scenes are hung on the walls next to prized antlers or a collection of beer mugs. Try some *Weisswürste* (white sausages) or hearty *Schweinebraten* (roast pork) with sauerkraut and *Knödel* (dumplings) while you soak up the atmosphere.

try the romantic 'Romeo and Juliet' breakfast for two, served until 4pm.
✚ K8 ✉ Franziskanerstrasse 4 ☎ 688 6043 🚇 S-Bahn Rosenheimer Platz

HUNDSKUGEL (€€)

Wind the clock back to the Middle Ages at Munich's oldest inn, dating from 1440.
✚ H7 ✉ Hotterstrasse 18 ☎ 26 42 72 🕐 Daily 10.30am–midnight 🚇 U- or S-Bahn Marienplatz

JOE PEÑA'S (€€)

www.joepenas.com
This Mexican restaurant is always packed due to its delicious fajitas, burritos and tequilas.
✚ J8 ✉ Buttermelcher-strasse 17 ☎ 22 64 63 🕐 Dinner only 5pm–1am

KÖNIGSHOF (€€€)

www.koenigshof-hotel.de
This gastronomic temple, in one of Munich's finest hotels, offers tempting regional delicacies and an extensive wine list in an elegant setting overlooking Karlsplatz.
✚ H7 ✉ Karlsplatz 25 ☎ 55 13 60 🕐 Closed Sun 🚇 U- or S-Bahn Karlsplatz

MAREDO (€€)

www.maredo.de
The best steak and salad in town is only a stone's throw from Marienplatz.
✚ J7 ✉ Tal 8 ☎ 29 46 61 🕐 Daily 11.30–11.30 🚇 U- or S-Bahn Marienplatz

MÜNCHNER SUPPENKÜCHE (€)

www.muenchner-suppenkueche.com

Try the *Pfannkuchen-suppe* (pancake soup) or *Leberknödelsuppe* (liver dumpling soup) at this soup kitchen.

➕ J7 ✉ Viktualienmarkt ☎ 2609 599 🕐 Shop hours 🚇 U- or S-Bahn Marienplatz

NORDSEE (€)

www.nordsee.de

This fast-food fish eatery offers a range of hot and cold dishes. There's standing room only.

➕ J7 ✉ Viktualienmarkt ☎ 22 11 86 🕐 Mon–Fri 8–7, Sat 8–4 🚇 U- or S-Bahn Marienplatz

NÜRNBERGER BRATWURST GLÖCKL (€)

www.bratwurst-gloeckl.de

An ancient tavern, best known for its *Nürnberger Bratwurst* (Nuremburg sausage), grilled over an open beechwood fire and served with sauerkraut.

➕ J7 ✉ Frauenplatz 9 ☎ 2919 450 🕐 Daily 10am–midnight 🚇 U- or S-Bahn Marienplatz

PRINZ MYSHKIN (€€)

www.prinzmyshkin.com

Trendy café with a menu of creative vegetarian dishes. Don't miss the tofu stroganoff or the *involtini,* chard roulades filled with nuts and tofu.

➕ J7 ✉ Hackenstrasse 2 ☎ 26 55 96 🕐 Daily 11.30–10.30 🚇 U- or S-Bahn Marienplatz

RATSKELLER (€€)

www.ratskeller.com

Good solid cuisine under the vaulted arches of the New Town Hall's cellar.

➕ J7 ✉ Marienplatz 8 ☎ 2199 890 🕐 Daily 10am–midnight 🚇 U- or S-Bahn Marienplatz

RUE DES HALLES (€€€)

Sophisticated, Parisian dining in fashionable Haidhausen.

➕ L8 ✉ Steinstrasse 18 ☎ 48 56 75 🕐 Dinner only 🚇 S-Bahn Rosenheimer Platz

SCHLEMMERMEYER (€)

Hearty Bavarian specialties, including *Weisswurst* and *Leberkäs,* served in big portions, with steaming mugs of glühwein in winter.

➕ J7 ✉ Viktualienmarkt

MAHLZEIT!

Mahlzeiten (mealtimes) are comparatively early in Munich, because most people start work early (around 7–8am). Lunch is eaten between 11.30 and 2 and is for many the main meal of the day, followed by a light supper or *Abendbrot* ('evening bread'). Restaurants usually serve dinner between 6.30 and 11pm when it is polite to wish fellow diners '*Guten Appetit*'. However, during the day it is more common to hear the word '*Mahlzeit*'.

🕐 Shop hours 🚇 U- or S-Bahn Marienplatz

VINAIOLO (€€)

www.vinaiolo.de

This top-notch Italian restaurant, located in fashionable Haidhausen, is reasonably priced.

➕ L8 ✉ Steinstrasse 42 ☎ 4895 0356 🕐 Sun–Fri noon–3, 6.30–1, Sat 6.30–1 🚇 S-Bahn Rosenheimer Platz 🚊 Tram 15, 25

VINCENZ MURR (€)

Help yourself at the extensive salad bar, then have a picnic by the fountain opposite.

➕ J7 ✉ Rosenstrasse 7 ☎ 260 4765 🕐 Shop hours 🚇 U- or S-Bahn Marienplatz

WEISSES BRÄUHAUS (€)

www.weisses-brauhaus.de

The *Weisswürste* here are easily the best in town, accompanied by a wickedly strong *Weissbier*.

➕ J7 ✉ Tal 7 ☎ 2901 380 🕐 Daily 8am–1am 🚇 U-or S-Bahn Marienplatz

ZUM ALTEN MARKT

www.zumaltenmarkt.de

An Alpine-style restaurant, all wood beams, is the setting for traditional Bavarian meat and fish dishes served in daunting quantities.

➕ J7 ✉ Dreifaltigkeitsplatz 3 (at Viktualienmarkt) ☎ 29 99 95 🕐 Mon–Sat 11am–midnight

Soak up the city's unique charm and atmosphere from the royal Residenz to the cobbled streets of the Altstadt surrounding the Hofbräuhaus, and browse in the city's most exclusive shops.

Sights	**46–53**	Top 25 **25**
Walk	**54**	Bayerisches Nationalmuseum ▷ **46**
Shopping	**55–56**	Hofbräuhaus ▷ **47**
		Nationaltheater ▷ **48**
Entertainment and Nightlife	**57**	Odeonsplatz ▷ **49**
		Residenz ▷ **50**
Restaurants	**58**	

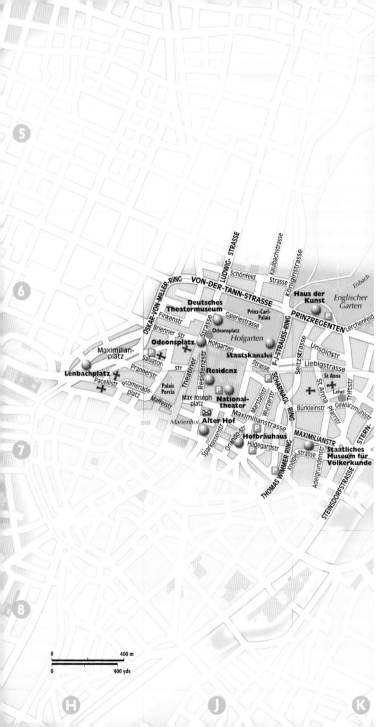

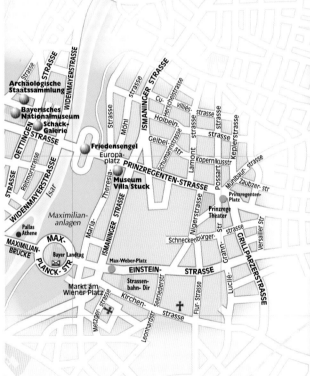

Archäologische
Staatssammlung

Bayerisches
Nationalmuseum

Schack-
Galerie

OETTINGEN
STRASSE

WIDENMAYERSTRASSE

STRASSE

Friedensengel

Europa-
platz

PRINZREGENTEN-STRASSE

Reitmorstrasse

WIDENMAYERSTRASSE

Isar

Maximilian-
anlagen

Pallas
Athene

MAXIMILIAN-
BRÜCKE

MAX-
PLANCK-STR.

Bayer. Landtag

Markt am
Wiener Platz

Metzgerstrasse

Museum
Villa Stuck

ISMANINGER STRASSE

Theresia-

Maria-

ISMANINGER STRASSE

Möhl

Herschelstrasse

villiés-
strasse

Holbein-

Geibel

Schumannstrasse

Lamont

Kopernikusstr.

strasse

Keplerstrasse

Possart

Mühlbaur- strasse

zauber- str.

Prinzregenten-
Platz

Niggerstrasse

Prinzrege
Theater

strasse

Grahn-

Schneckenburger-

str.

Versailler Str.

GRILLPARZERSTRASSE

Max-Weber-Platz

EINSTEIN-

STRASSE

Strassen-
bahn- Dir

Seeriederstr.

Kirchen-

strasse

Flur Strasse

Lucile-

Leonhardtstr.

Bayerisches Nationalmuseum

The Bavarian National Museum was founded by Maximilian II in the 19th century

THE BASICS

www.bayerisches-national museum.de

✚ K6

✉ Prinzregentenstrasse 3

☎ 211 24 01

🕐 Tue–Sun 10–5 (Thu until 8pm)

🚇 U-Bahn Lehel

🚌 100; tram 17

♿ Good

💰 Moderate; Sun inexpensive

HIGHLIGHTS

● 16th- century model of Munich, by master wood-carver Jakob Sandtner
● Augsburg Weaving Room
● Tilman Riemenschneider sculptures
● Crib collection
● Flanders Tapestry Room
● Weaponry Room
● Closet from Palais Tattenbach

The Bavarian National Museum is one of Europe's leading museums of folk art, and is guaranteed to give you a real taste of Bavarian life over the centuries to the present day.

Wittelsbach treasures Thanks to the Wittelsbach rulers' passion for collecting works of art, this museum was founded in 1885 by Maximilian II and transferred to its present site in 1900. Even the building mirrors the various periods represented within the museum: the west wing is Romanesque, the east wing Renaissance, the tower baroque and the west end rococo. The interior is divided into two main collections—Folklore and Art History—providing a comprehensive survey of German cultural history, both sacred and secular, from the early Middle Ages to the present.

Folklore A series of rooms authentically decorated with rustic Bavarian furniture, glass, pottery and woodcraft provides a wonderful insight into the country life of bygone years. The Augsburg Room, with its outstanding carved ceiling, is particularly attractive. The museum is famous for its sculptures by Hans Leinberger, Ignaz Günther and Tilman Riemenschneider and its large crib collection.

Art history This collection consists of a series of specialist departments including Bavarian *Trachten* (traditional costume), tapestries, porcelain, jewellery, armour and the largest ivory collection in Europe.

Hofbräuhaus is the home of Bavarian beer

Hofbräuhaus

TOP 25

No trip to Munich is complete without a visit to the Hofbräuhaus, despite its being a tourist honeypot, to sip a cool beer in the shady courtyard or in the lively beer hall. The Hofbräuhaus was founded by Wilhelm V in 1589.

Royal beer The brewery produced a special dark ale for Wilhelm's court, because he disliked the expensive local beer. Beer in Bavaria had been considered an aristocratic drink ever since the harsh winters of the 14th century destroyed the Bavarian vineyards. The ordinary citizens were unable to taste this royal brew until 1828, when the brewery finally became an inn.

Battle of the Hofbräuhaus The first mass meeting of the National Socialist Workers' Party (later the Nazi Party) was held in the Hofbräuhaus in 1920. It soon became regarded as the city's most prestigious political beer-hall arena. Here Hitler established himself as a powerful orator. On 4 November 1921, his storm troops first gained notoriety in a huge brawl, later known as the *Schlacht im Hofbräuhaus* (Battle of the Hofbräuhaus). Despite the hurling of chairs and beer mugs, Hitler managed to finish his speech.

World's most famous pub Undoubtedly the city's best-known institution after the Oktoberfest, and a meeting place for visitors from all over the world, the Hofbräuhaus—with its long tables, buxom dirndl-clad waitresses and jolly Bavarian music—is a must for tourists.

THE BASICS

www.hofbraeuhaus.de

✚ J7

✉ Am Platzl 9

☎ 2901 3610

🕐 Daily 9am–11.30pm. Brass band 11am–3pm, 5.30–midnight

Ⓤ U- or S-Bahn Marienplatz

🚌 52, 131; tram 19

♿ Good

DID YOU KNOW?

● The Hofbräuhaus is the world's most famous pub.
● The Munich Beer Regulations of 1487 are the oldest written food laws in the world.
● Bavaria is home to some 600 breweries.
● The Hofbräuhaus has its very own drinking song: *'In München steht ein Hofbräuhaus, eins, zwei, drei, g'soffa'…*(one, two, three and down the hatch).

INNENSTADT NORD

TOP 25

Nationaltheater

 TOP 25

The fully restored Nationaltheater, inside and out

Munich's Nationaltheater ranks among the world's leading opera houses. One of the few German theatres to have been restored to its magnificent pre-war grandeur, it is definitely worth the visit, even if opera is not your scene.

HIGHLIGHTS

Outside
● Façade
● Pediment with Apollo and the Muses, Georg Brenninger, 1972
● Pediment with glass mosaic of *Pegasus with the Horae*, Leo Schwanthaler, 19th century

Inside
● Auditorium
● Royal box
● High-tech stage machinery and backstage equipment
● Prompter's box
● Foyer

People's opera house The Nationaltheater has been home to the world-famous Bayerische Staatsoper (Bavarian State Opera) since 1818. After wartime bombing its distinguished Greek-temple design with a simple colonnaded façade stood in ruins for years until a group of citizens raised sufficient funds to restore it to its former glory. It was reopened in 1963.

Behind the scenes Most days at 2pm, during a fascinating tour, it is possible to take a rare glimpse backstage. The grandiose auditorium, with five tiers of seating decorated in plush red, gold, ivory and dove blue, is crowned by an enormous chandelier, which magically disappears into the ceiling when the curtain rises. The impressive 'Greek' foyer rooms provide an elegant setting for the audience to promenade in their finery.

Opening nights Many important operas have been premiered here over the centuries, including five by Wagner during the reign of Ludwig II, and many eminent artists have conducted, directed and performed here in a repertoire ranging from traditional Munich favourites—Mozart, Wagner and Strauss—to new commissions from contemporary German composers.

Odeonsplatz

Monumental buildings surround this spacious square at the start of the city's two finest boulevards. Rubbing the noses of the lions guarding the entrance to the Residenz is said to bring good luck.

Grand plan for urban expansion Ludwig I entrusted the layout of Odeonsplatz to Leo von Klenze in the early 19th century to demonstrate the wealth of his flourishing kingdom. It also shows Klenze's passion for Renaissance Italy. His neoclassical Leuchtenberg-Palais (today the Bavarian Ministry of Finance) was inspired by Rome's Palazzo Farnese, and set the pattern for the development of the magnificent Ludwigstrasse.

Feldherrnhalle Apart from the striking Theatinerkirche—Bavaria's first baroque building and for many the most beautiful church in Munich—perhaps the most imposing building in Odeonsplatz is the Feldherrnhalle (Military Commander's Hall). It was commissioned by Ludwig I, and designed by Freidrich von Gärtner as a tribute to the Bavarian army, and adorned with statues of Bavarian generals. Note the faces of the two bronze lions: one is said to be growling at the Residenz while the other, facing the church, remains silent.

The Court Garden The peaceful Hofgarten—a park beside Odeonsplatz—retains its original 17th-century Italian layout of beautifully tended flowerbeds and fountains.

THE BASICS

⊞ J6
🍴 Hofgarten Café
🚇 U-Bahn Odeonsplatz
🚌 100

HIGHLIGHTS

- Theatinerkirche
- Feldherrnhalle
- Hofgarten
- Leuchtenberg-Palais
- Odeon
- Ludwig I monument
- Preysing Palais
- Staatskanzlei (▷ 53)

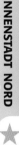

INNENSTADT NORD

TOP 25

49

Residenz

HIGHLIGHTS

● Cuvilliés Theatre
● Schatzkammer
● Antiquarium
● Ahnengalerie
● Hofkapelle
● Egyptian Art Museum
● Coin Museum

TIP

● Try to attend one of the summer open-air concerts at the Residenz, held in the atmospheric Brunnenhof courtyard. Contact München Ticket (tel: 0180 5481 8181).

The glittering state rooms of this magnificent palace demonstrate the power and wealth of the Wittelsbach dynasty—five centuries of dukes, prince-electors and kings.

Historical evolution Despite devastating damage in World War II, the Residenz was painstakingly reconstructed over four decades to its original state: a harmonious fusion of Renaissance, baroque, rococo and neoclassical styles. As you explore the 112 grand rooms crammed with priceless treasures, you can trace the centuries of architectural development, as well as the history and lifestyles of the great Wittelsbach family dynasty.

Palace highlights It would take a full day to see everything; if time is limited just see the

Munich's former ducal palace and gardens, the Residenz and Hofgarten, were begun by the Wittelsbachs in 1385 and contain the Antiquarium, the oldest German museum of Greek antiquities

Ahnengalerie (Ancestral Portrait Gallery), hung with paintings of 121 members of the Wittelsbach family; the Hofkapelle and the Reiche Kapelle, two intimate chapels (one for the courtiers and the other for the royal family); the Brunnenhof courtyard with its magnificent fountain; the unusual shell-encrusted Grottenhof courtyard; and the Antiquarium, the largest Renaissance vaulted hall in northern Europe.

Jewel in the crown The restored Cuvilliés-Theater, jewel of the Residenz and the world's finest rococo theatre, is a dazzling spectacle. Built in 1750, it hosted the première of Mozart's *Idomeneo* in 1781. Also, visit the Schatzkammer (Treasury) to see the crown jewels and one of the most valuable collections of ecclesiastical and secular treasures in Europe, spanning a thousand years.

THE BASICS

www.residenz-
muenchen.de

⊞ J7

✉ Residenzstrasse/
Max-Joseph-Platz 3

☎ 29 06 71

🕐 Daily 10–4 (6 in summer)

Ⓤ U- or S-Bahn
Marienplatz, U-Bahn
Odeonsplatz

🚌 100; tram 19

♿ Good

💷 Moderate

More to See

ALTER HOF

www.alter-hof-muenchen.de

With its picturesque tower, oriel window and cobbled courtyard, the Alter Hof was the royal residence (and home to the German Emperor, Ludwig IV from 1328) from the late 12th century until the Residenz was built in the late 14th century. Today, part of the complex contains the popular 'Vinorant' restaurant and wine cellar.

➕ J7 ✉ Burgstrasse 8 🚇 U-Bahn Marienplatz

ARCHÄOLOGISCHE STAATSSAMMLUNG

www.archaeologie-bayern.de

The Archaeological Collection focuses on the periods from the Early Stone Age to the Middle Ages, exhibiting everyday possessions, sacred art and burial objects discovered in Bavaria.

➕ K6 ✉ Lerchenfeldstrasse 2
☎ 211 2402 🕐 Tue–Sun 9.30–5.30
🚇 U-Bahn Lehel 🚃 Tram 17
💰 Inexpensive

DEUTSCHES THEATERMUSEUM

www.stmwfk.bayern.de

This small but fascinating display of set designs, costumes, photographs and props brings Germany's rich theatrical past to life.

➕ J6 ✉ Galeriestrasse 4a ☎ 2106 9128
🕐 Tue–Sun 10–4 🚇 U-Bahn Odeonsplatz
💰 Moderate

FRIEDENSENGEL

The golden Angel of Peace, perched high above the River Isar, was built for the 25th anniversary of Germany's victory over France in 1871.

➕ L6 ✉ Prinzregentenstrasse 🚌 100; tram 18

HAUS DER KUNST

www.hausderkunst.de

This monstrous Nazi building—one of the few that Allied bombardments missed—was nicknamed the *Weisswurst* (white sausage) gallery by Hitler's opponents, because of its crude neoclassical columns. This immense, pseudo-Classical building, designed by Paul Ludwig Troost, was

Artwork in the Haus der Kunst

The golden figure of the Friedensengel (Angel of Peace)

the first monumental Nazi building in Munich, and set the pattern for later designs. Today, its lofty interior provides an impressive forum for major modern art exhibitions.

➕ K6 ✉ Prinzregentenstrasse 1 ☎ 2112 7113 🕐 Daily 10–8 (Thu until 10) 🚇 U-Bahn Lehel 🚌 100; tram 17 💵 Varies: moderate to expensive

LENBACHPLATZ

In this busy square is Munich's loveliest neoclassical fountain (1895). Its two figures symbolize the destructive and healing power of water.

➕ H6 ✉ Lenbachplatz 🚇 U-Bahn Karlsplatz

MUSEUM VILLA STUCK

www.villastuck.de

This stunning Jugendstil villa, the former home of artist Franz von Stuck, has been beautifully restored and contains changing exhibitions dedicated to 20th-century art.

➕ L7 ✉ Prinzregentenstrasse 60 ☎ 4555 5125 🕐 Tue–Sun 11–6 🚌 100; tram 18 🚇 U-Bahn Prinzregentenplatz 💵 Inexpensive

SCHACK-GALERIE

www.pinakothek.de

This intimate gallery captures the artistic spirit of 19th-century German art.

➕ K6 ✉ Prinzregentenstrasse 9 ☎ 238 0520 🕐 Tue–Sun 10–5 🚌 100; tram 18 🚇 U-Bahn Lehel 💵 Inexpensive

STAATSKANZLEI

The gleaming glass and steel Bavarian State Chancellery building is framed by a Renaissance-style arcade and has the dome of the former Army Museum as its focal point.

➕ J6 ✉ Hofgarten 🚇 U-Bahn Odeonsplatz

STAATLICHES MUSEUM FÜR VÖLKERKUNDE

www.voelkerkundemuseum-muenchen.de

This huge, fascinating museum of ethnography holds 150,000 exhibits, displayed by region—South America, Africa, India, Oceania and the Islamic Orient.

➕ K7 ✉ Maximilianstrasse 42 ☎ 210 1361 00 🕐 Tue–Sun 9.30–5.30 🍴 Café 🚇 U-Bahn Lehel 💵 Moderate

The Renaissance-style arcade of the Staatskanzlei

Royal Munich

Wind the clocks back and stroll through Royal Munich with its maze of attractive cobbled streets and royal residences.

DISTANCE: 1.3km (0.8 miles) **ALLOW:** 1 hour (excluding visits)

START

ODEONSPLATZ (▷ 49)
🞧 J6 🔵 U-Bahn Odeonsplatz

END

ENGLISCHER GARTEN (▷ 64–65)
🞧 K4 🔵 U-Bahn Universität

① From Odeonsplatz walk down Theatinerstrasse, with its glitzy boutiques. Turn left at Marien-hof then first right into Dienerstrasse past Alois Dallmayr—the former royal delicatessen—to Marienplatz (▷ 28–29).

⑧ The famous Englischer Garten (English Garden) (▷ 64–65) is just a stone's throw from the gallery. Head towards the Love Temple, one of the park's great landmarks, for splendid views of Munich's skyline.

② From the Old Town Hall (▷ 32), go down Burgstrasse (beside Beck department store), the oldest street in the city, past homes of former residents Mozart and Cuvilliés.

⑦ Cut diagonally across the gardens, past the Staatskanzlei (▷ 53), finished in 1994, and continue down a narrow path alongside the Dichtergarten (Poets' Garden). Cross Von-der-Tann-Strasse by the pedestrian subway to the Haus der Kunst (▷ 52).

③ Go through the archway of the old royal residence (Alter Hof ▷ 52) and turn right past the Central Mint (Münzhof) along Pfisterstrasse to soak up some true Bavarian atmosphere at the Hofbräuhaus (▷ 47).

⑥ Head up Residenzstrasse, past the Residenz (▷ 50–51) on your right. Returning to Odeonsplatz, head eastwards into the enchanting Hofgarten (Court Garden), with its fountains and formal flowerbeds.

④ On leaving the main entrance of the Hofbräuhaus, turn right through Platzl and past Am Kosttor up to the bright lights and dazzling designer windows of exclusive Maximilianstrasse.

⑤ Turn left at Maximilianstrasse towards the magnificently illuminated Nationaltheater (▷ 48) at Max-Joseph-Platz.

Shopping

ANTIKE UHREN EDER

www.uhreneder.ch

The silence of this beautiful shop is broken only by the ticking of valuable German timepieces dating from the 19th and early 20th centuries. A must for collectors.

➕ J6 ✉ Prannerstrasse 4
☎ 22 03 05 🚇 U- or S-Bahn Karlsplatz

BEHRINGER

www.behringer-schuhe.de

Fine shoes and accessories for men and women, from Prada to Jimmy Choo, in one of Germany's top shoe shops.

➕ J6 ✉ Salvatorplatz 4
☎ 29 59 55 🚇 U-Bahn Odeonsplatz

BOETTNER

One of Munich's oldest hostelries is well known for its schnapps, caviar and other delicacies.

➕ J7 ✉ Pfisterstrasse 9
☎ 22 12 10 🚇 U- or S-Bahn Marienplatz

BOGNER

This classic Munich company sells everything from sports clothes to traditional costumes for both men and women.

➕ J7 ✉ Residenzstrasse 14–15 ☎ 290 7040
🚇 U- or S-Bahn Marienplatz

BREE

www.bree.com

Smart suitcases, belts, handbags and more.

➕ J6 ✉ Theatinerhof, Salvatorstrasse 2 ☎ 29 87 45
🚇 U-Bahn Odeonplatz

BUTLERS

www.butlers-international.de

A fun shop, full of tempting ideas for holiday gifts, including fun household gadgets and knick-knacks.

➕ J7 ✉ Theatinerstrasse 14, Fünf Höfe ☎ 2423 1293
🚇 U-Bahn Odeonsplatz

DALLMAYR

www.dallmayr.de

Alois Dallmayr, the city's top delicatessen, famed for its mouth-watering displays, used to supply the Bavarian royal family. The first floor serves a lovely champagne breakfast.

➕ J7 ✉ Dienerstrasse 14–15
☎ 23501 🚇 U- or S-Bahn Marienplatz

DERSTET SINNE

www.ludwigbeck.com

This branch of the Ludwig

CELEBRATING IN STYLE

When Paul and Elsa Käfer opened a modest food and wine shop in Munich in 1930, they had no idea that their name (▷ 56, 58) would become synonymous with the stylish parties that their son would arrange, in the more prosperous 1960s, for film stars and other prominent members of post-war high society. The shop remains a food-lover's paradise and the catering business supplies such establishments as the roof-top restaurant of the Reichstag (German parliament building) in Berlin.

Beck department store specializes in exotic and extravagant bath and beauty products to pamper the weariest shopper.

➕ J7 ✉ Dienerstrasse 20
☎ 23 69 10 🚇 U- or S-Bahn Marienplatz

EDUARD MEIER

www.edmeier.de

Munich's oldest shoe shop, established in 1596, with leather sofas and first-class service.

➕ J7 ✉ Residenzstrasse 22
☎ 22 00 44 🚇 U- or S-Bahn Marienplatz

EILLES

www.eilles.de

One of several Eilles shops, selling fine tea, coffee and wines.

➕ J7 ✉ Residenzstrasse 13
☎ 22 61 84 🚇 U- or S-Bahn Marienplatz

ELLY SEIDL

www.ellyseidl.de

A tiny chocolate shop, famous for its pralines and its *Münchner Kuppeln* chocolates, which look like the onion-domes of the Frauenkirche.

➕ J7 ✉ Am Kosttor 2
☎ 22 15 22 🚇 U- or S-Bahn Marienplatz

FANSHOP

www.fcbayern.t-com.de

Everything imaginable for FC Bayern supporters, from scarves and teddies to clothing and sports bags.

➕ J7 ✉ Orlandostrasse 1 and 8 ☎ 24 38 69
🚇 U- or S-Bahn Marienplatz

INNENSTADT NORD

SHOPPING

55

FEINKOST KÄFER
www.feinkost-kaefer.de
An epicurean labyrinth selling food and drink from around the world in the smart Bogenhausen district.
➕ L7 ✉ Prinzregentenstrasse 73 ☎ 4 16 80 🚇 U-Bahn Prinzregentenplatz

HEMMERLE
www.hemmerle.de
The treasures in this traditional Munich jeweller are expensive but very solid.
➕ J7 ✉ Maximilianstrasse 14 ☎ 242 2600 🚋 Tram 19

KOKON
www.kokon.com
A magical blend of artefacts, fabrics and furnishings from around the world, with an impressive collection of garden furniture and exotic flowers.
➕ H6 ✉ Lenbach-Palais, Lenbachplatz 3 ☎ 552 5140 🚋 Tram 27

KUNSTGEWERBE-VEREIN
www.kunsthandwerk-bkv.de
Shop here for high-quality, carved, painted and handcrafted Bavarian products. Choose from puppets and pottery to jewellery and bright carnival masks—truly exclusive gifts.
➕ H7 ✉ Pacellistrasse 6–8 ☎ 290 1470 🚇 U- or S-Bahn Karlsplatz

LODEN-FREY
www.loden-frey.de
Choose your *Trachten* (Bavarian folk costume) from an endless selection here at the world's largest store for national costume. Children will love the toboggan run from the street level to the basement.
➕ J7 ✉ Maffeistrasse 7–9 ☎ 21 03 90 🚇 U- or S-Bahn Marienplatz

MARKT AM WIENER PLATZ
www.markt-am-wiener-platz.de
Tiny green wooden produce stands huddle around the maypole in Haidhausen—an attractive alternative to the supermarket.
➕ L7 ✉ Wiener Platz 🚇 U-Bahn Max-Weber-Platz

PORZELLAN-MANUFAKTUR NYMPHENBURG
www.nymphenburg.com
This famous porcelain manufacturer still turns out traditional rococo

designs. It is based in Nymphenburg Palace, with this outlet in the heart of the city.
➕ J6 ✉ Odeonsplatz 1 ☎ 28 24 28 🕐 Mon–Fri 10–5 🚇 U-Bahn Odeonsplatz

ROSENTHAL STUDIO-HAUS
www.rosenthal-studio-haus.de
Smart, contemporary Rosenthal porcelain and glass, together with other choice designer ware.
➕ J7 ✉ Dienerstrasse 17 ☎ 22 26 17 🚇 U- or S-Bahn Marienplatz

SCHREIBMAYR
www.kaut-bullinger.de
Beautiful desk equipment, handmade paper and pens for lovers of the art of letter writing, together with ink in every imaginable shade, including 'King Ludwig's ink'.
➕ J7 ✉ Theatinerstrasse 11 (in den Fünf Höfen) ☎ 219 9840 🚇 U- or S-Bahn Marienplatz

THERESA
www.mytheresa.com
Trendy and wildly expensive designer fashions, mainly Italian prêt-à-porter.
➕ J7 ✉ Maffeistrasse 3 ☎ 22 48 45 🚇 U-Bahn Odeonsplatz

Entertainment and Nightlife

CUVILLIÉS-THEATER
www.residenz-muenchen.de
Considered the finest rococo theatre in the world, popular for both opera and drama. Currently closed for renovation work.
✚ J7 ✉ Residenzstrasse 1 ☎ 29 68 36 Ⓤ U-Bahn Odeonsplatz

HERKULESSAAL
www.residenz-muenchen.de
Munich's most impressive concert hall, in the Residenz.
✚ J7 ✉ Residenzstrasse 1 ☎ 29 06 71 Ⓤ U-Bahn Odeonsplatz

JAZZCLUB UNTERFAHRT
www.unterfahrt.de
One of Europe's most important jazz clubs featuring modern jazz and avant-garde names.
✚ L7 ✉ Einsteinstrasse 42 ☎ 448 2794 Ⓒ Sun–Thu 7.30pm–1am, Fri–Sat 7.30pm–3am Ⓤ U-Bahn Max-Weber-Platz 🚋 Tram 19

JODLERWIRT
www.jodlerwirt-muenchen.net
This tiny, folksy bar is straight out of the Bavarian countryside—always crowded and jolly, often with local yodellers at night.
✚ J7 ✉ Altenhofstrasse 4 ☎ 22 12 49 Ⓒ Mon–Sat 7pm–3am Ⓤ U- or S-Bahn Marienplatz

KOMÖDIE IM BAYERISCHEN HOF
www.komoedie-muenchen.de
Sophisticated light comedy is the specialty here.
✚ H7 ✉ Promenadeplatz 6 ☎ 16 05 30 Ⓤ U- or S-Bahn Karlsplatz

MÜNCHNER KAMMERSPIELE
www.muenchner-kammer-spiele.de
The 'Munich Playhouse' is considered one of Germany's best theatres. Tickets are like gold dust.
✚ J7 ✉ Falkenbergstrasse 2 ☎ 2339 6600 Ⓤ U- or S-Bahn Marienplatz

NATIONALTHEATER
www.staatstheater.bayern.de
www.bayerische.staatsoper.de
The home of the Bavarian State Opera (▷ 48) is one of Europe's most respected opera houses. The excellent opera festival in July is the high point of

MUSICAL MECCA
Munich and music go hand-in-hand. The city's connection with Mozart, Wagner and Richard Strauss, not to mention its three symphony orchestras, has made it famous throughout the world. Today, it plays host to major events in the musical calendar including the glamorous Opera Festival and the Summer Concert Season at Nymphenburg Palace.

Munich's cultural year.
✚ J7 ✉ Max-Joseph-Platz ☎ 2185 1920 Ⓤ U- or S-Bahn Marienplatz

P1
www.p1-club.de
Extremely chic club in the basement of the Haus der Kunst (▷ 52). Eight different bars frequented by models and celebrities.
✚ K6 ✉ Prinzregenten-strasse 1 ☎ 211 1140 Ⓒ 11pm–4am Ⓤ U-Bahn Lehel

PRINZREGENTEN-THEATER
www.prinzregententheater.de
Originally built to emulate the famous Wagner Festspielhaus in Bayreuth in 1900. Today it stages plays, concerts, opera and musicals.
✚ L7 ✉ Prinzregentenplatz 12 ☎ 2185 2899 Ⓤ U-Bahn Prinzregentenplatz

SCHUMANN'S
www.schumanns.de
It's hard to get a table here at Germany's number-one bar, but once inside you can enjoy watching Munich's 'Schickeria' (chic set) at play.
✚ J6 ✉ Odeonsplatz 6–7 ☎ 22 90 60 Ⓒ Mon–Fri 5pm–3am, Sun 6pm–3am 🚋 Tram 19

Restaurants

BOGENHAUSER HOF (€€€)

www.bogenhauser-hof.de
This small countrified restaurant is located in a picture-book house. Reservations are essential if you wish to sample the inspired French-style cuisine and attentive service.
🔢 L7 ✉ Ismaninger Strasse 85 ☎ 98 55 86 🕐 Mon–Fri 12–4pm, 6pm–1am 🚋 Tram 18

CAFÉ WIENER PLATZ (€)

www.cafewienerplatz.de
A chic crowd frequents this modern coffeehouse with its extensive breakfast menu.
🔢 L7 ✉ Innere-Wiener-Strasse 48 ☎ 448 9494 🚋 Tram 19

DUKATZ IM LITERATURHAUS (€)

www.dukatz.de
This airy, modern café attracts an arty set for weekly poetry readings.
🔢 J7 ✉ Maffeistrasse 3a ☎ 7104 07373 🕐 Mon–Sat 10am–1am, Sun 10–7 🚇 U- or S-Bahn

EISBACH (€€–€€€)

www.eisbach.biz
A chic, modern bar with delicious, bagels, pastries, pancakes and freshly squeezed juices served alfresco in summer.
🔢 J7 ✉ Marstallplatz 3 ☎ 2280 1680 🕐 Daily 10am–1am 🚋 Tram 19

HALALI (€€€)

www.restaurant-halali.de
Halali's secret is good, unpretentious, regional home cooking.
🔢 J6 ✉ Schönfeldstrasse 22 ☎ 28 59 09 🕐 Mon–Fri lunch, dinner, Sat dinner only 🚇 U-Bahn Odeonsplatz

HAXNBAUER IM SCHOLASTIKAHAUS (€€)

www.kuffler-gastronomie.de
Watch the cooks turning giant shanks of pork (Schweinshax'n) over open beechwood fires in this ancient inn. Huge, portions for meat lovers.
🔢 J7 ✉ Sparkassenstrasse ☎ 216 6540 🕐 Daily 11am–midnight 🚇 U- or S-Bahn Marienplatz

LEBKUCHEN TRADITION

The 600-year-old tradition of baking Lebkuchen is thought to derive from recipes concocted by medieval monks. The biscuits (cookies), are flavoured primarily with almonds, honey and spices. The pre-Christmas season is the busiest time for Lebkuchen producer Schmidt when up to 3 million biscuits are made every day.

KÄFER-SCHÄNKE (€€€)

www.feinkost-kaefer.de
This warren of rooms above the famous Käfer delicatessen promises a gastronomic experience with creative dishes and a lavish buffet.
🔢 L7 ✉ Prinzregentenstrasse 73 ☎ 41 68 247 🕐 Mon–Sat 11.30am–1am 🚇 U-Bahn Prinzregentenplatz

KEMPINSKI HOTEL VIER JAHRESZEITEN (€€)

www.kempinski-vierjahreszeiten.com
One of Munich's top hotels serves a traditional English afternoon tea.
🔢 J7 ✉ Maximilianstrasse 17 ☎ 21 250 🕐 Daily 2–6 🚇 U-Bahn Odeonsplatz 🚋 Tram 19

SPATENHAUS AN DER OPER (€€)

www.kuffler-gastronomie.de
Top-notch Bavarian cuisine opposite the opera and popular with the after-theatre crowd.
🔢 J7 ✉ Residenzstrasse 12 ☎ 290 7060 🕐 Daily 11.30am–12.30am 🚇 U- or S-Bahn Marienplatz

TRADER VIC'S (€€€)

www.bayerischerhof.de
A varied Polynesian menu ranging from wonton soup to barbecued spare ribs or Calcutta lobster.
🔢 H7 ✉ Hotel Bayerischer Hof, Promenadeplatz 2–6 ☎ 212 0995 🕐 Daily 5pm–3am 🚇 U- or S-Bahn Marienplatz

Art treasures abound in the tranquil Max suburb, with its many museums and galleries. Trendy Schwabing, beside the Englischer Garten and the university, buzzes with boutiques, bars and restaurants.

Sights	62–72	Top 25	**25**
Walk	73	Alte Pinakothek ▷ **62**	
		Englischer Garten ▷ **64**	
Shopping	74–75	Königsplatz ▷ **66**	
		Lenbachhaus ▷ **68**	
Entertainment and Nightlife	76	Neue Pinakothek ▷ **69**	
		Pinakothek der Moderne ▷ **70**	
Restaurants	77–78		

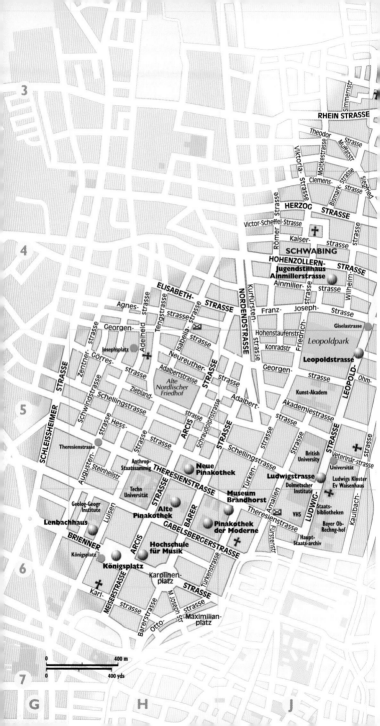

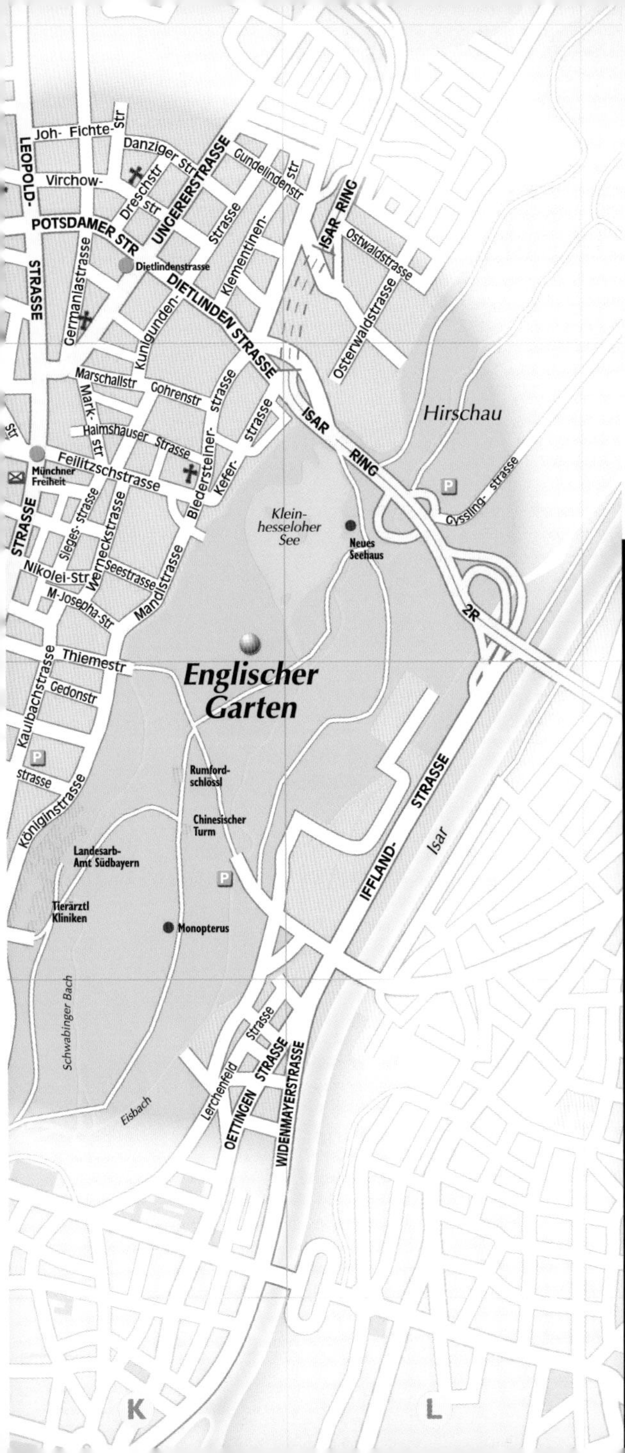

LEOPOLD-
STRASSE

Joh.- Fichte- str

Danziger str

Virchow-

POTSDAMER STR

UNGERERSTRASSE

Dreschstr

Gundelindenstr str

ISAR - RING

Ostwaldstrasse

Germaniastrasse

Dietlindenstrasse

DIETLINDEN STRASSE

Klementinen- str

STRASSE

Klementinenstrasse

Osterwaldstrasse

Marschallstr

Gohrenstr

Kunigunden- strasse

Biedersteiner- strasse

Kefer- strasse

ISAR

RING

Hirschau

Haimhauser Strasse

Münchner
Freiheit

Feilitzschstrasse

P

Cossling- strasse

Mark-str

STRASSE

Sieges- strasse

Neckerstr

Esseestrasse

Mandlstrasse

Klein-
hesseloher
See

Neues
Seehaus

Nikolei-Str

M-Josepha-Str

2R

Kaulbachstrasse

Thiemestr

Gedonstr

strasse

**Englischer
Garten**

Königinstrasse

P

Rumford-
schlössl

Chinesischer
Turm

IFFLAND-

STRASSE

Isar

Landesarb-
Amt Südbayern

Tierärztl
Kliniken

P

Monopterus

Schwabinger Bach

Eisbach

Lerchenfeld strasse

STRASSE

OETTINGEN

WIDENMAYERSTRASSE

K

L

The Old Masters are the highlight at this art gallery

Alte Pinakothek

With more than 850 Old Master paintings, this massive museum, the Old Picture Gallery, is rated alongside the Louvre, Uffizi, Prado and the Metropolitan as one of the world's most important galleries. The Rubens Collection alone is the finest on earth.

Architectural masterpiece The pinnacle of Bavaria's centuries-old dedication to the arts, the gallery was commissioned by Ludwig I and designed by Leo von Klenze to replace the older Kammergalerie in the Residenz, which had become too small for the Royal Collection. Fashioned on the Renaissance palaces of Venice, it took 10 years to construct and on completion in 1836 was proclaimed a masterpiece—the largest gallery building of its time and a model for other museum buildings in Rome and Brussels. During World War II it was so badly damaged that demolition of the site was contemplated. Restored in the 1950s and given an extensive facelift in the 1990s, the magnificent gallery provides a fitting backdrop for one of the world's finest collections of Western paintings.

Priceless treasures All the main schools of European art from the Middle Ages to the beginning of the 19th century are represented, with the emphasis on German, Dutch and Flemish paintings, including works by Dürer, van Dyck, Rembrandt and Breughel, and more than 100 pieces by Rubens (the finest collection of its kind in the world).

THE BASICS

www.alte-pinakothek.de

🕂 H6

✉ Barer Strasse 27

☎ 23 80 52 16

🕐 Tue 10–8, Wed—Sun 10–6

🚇 U-Bahn Theresienstrasse

🚋 Tram 27

♿ Very good

🍴 Moderate

HIGHLIGHTS

● *Fool's Paradise*, Pieter Breughel the Elder
● *Four Apostles*, Dürer
● *Adoration of the Magi*, Tiepolo
● *Madonna Tempi*, Raphael
● *The Great Last Judgement*, Rubens
● *The Resurrection*, Rembrandt

HIGHLIGHTS

- Chinese Tower
- Kleinhesseloher See and Seehaus
- Monopteros
- Japanese Tea House (tea ceremonies on the second weekend of every month Apr–end Oct)
- Rumford House

TIP

- Enjoy a piping-hot cup of *glühwein*, served at the Chinese Tower in winter!

The English Garden ranks highly on every Münchner's list of preferred city spots. On a sunny day, there's nothing more enjoyable than a stroll in this vast, idyllic park, full of people from all walks of life.

Munich's 'green lung' People come here to enjoy themselves – families boating, musicians busking, children feeding the ducks, New Age groups gathered by the love temple, professionals picnicking in their lunch break, jolly crowds in the packed beer gardens. For this is Munich's beloved 'green lung'—373ha (920 acres) of parkland stretching over 5km (3 miles) along the River Isar, and one of the largest city parks in the world.

English influences The English Garden was created by Count Rumford and Ludwig von Sckell in

The Englischer Garten was Europe's first people's park and is still hugely popular today

1789. Breaking away from the French style of manicured lawns and geometrical flowerbeds, they transformed the Wittelsbach hunting ground into an informal, countrified Volksgarten (people's park).

Attractions Start at the Kleinhesseloher See, an artificial lake with boats for rent. Or spend time relaxing at the Seehaus beer garden before heading south toward the Monopteros, a circular, Greek-style love temple with a splendid view of the park and the distant spires of old Munich. As well as English and Greek influences, the park also has a distinctive oriental tone with its Japanese Tea House and Chinese Tower. It also marks the city's most famous beer garden—popular for its brass band, old-fashioned children's merry-go-round and permanent *Oktoberfest* atmosphere.

THE BASICS

www.schloesser.bayern.de

🔳 K4

🕙 Dawn–dusk

🍴 Chinese Tower beer garden, Seehaus restaurant and beer garden (▷ 78), Japanese Tea House, Aumeister restaurant and beer garden

🚇 U-Bahn Odeonsplatz, Universität, Giselastrasse, Münchner Freiheit

🚌 100, 144, 180, 181, 187, 231, 232; tram 17

🚤 Rowing boats for hire at Kleinhesseloher See in summer

Königsplatz

HIGHLIGHTS

Glyptothek
- Barberini Faun
- Mnesarete tomb relief
- Aeginetan marbles
- Boy with a goose

Staatliche Antikensammlung
- Exekias' Dionysus cup
- Golden funerary wreath from Armento

TIP

- There are free guided tours of the museums, on Wednesdays at 6pm for the Staatliche Antikensammlung, and on Thursdays at 6pm for the Glyptothek.

This majestic square, nicknamed 'Athens-on-the-Isar', and flanked by three immense neoclassical temples, may come as a surprise in the heart of Munich.

The Square and the Propyläen Along with the buildings of Ludwigstrasse, Königsplatz represents Ludwig I's greatest contribution to Munich. Laid out by Leo von Klenze, according to plans created by Carl von Fischer, the square took 50 years to complete, from 1812 to 1862. The final building, the Propyläen, fashioned after the entrance to the Athenian Acropolis, is the most striking.

Nazi control Between 1933 and 1935, the appearance of Königsplatz was completely transformed. Hitler paved over the grassy, tree-lined

The Glyptothek (Sculpture Museum) and Staatliche Antikensammlung (State Collection of Antiquities) on Königsplatz

square and Königsplatz became the National Socialists' 'Akropolis Germaniae'—a setting for Nazi rallies. The paving stones have been replaced by broad expanses of lawn, enabling Königsplatz to return to its former serenity.

Museums The Glyptothek, or Sculpture Museum, on the north flank of Königsplatz is the oldest museum in Munich and one of the most celebrated neoclassical buildings in Germany. Inside is one of Europe's foremost collections of ancient Greek and Roman sculpture. Look out for the crowned bust of Emperor Augustus and the mosaic terrace depicting Aion from Sentinum. To the south, the Corinthian-style Staatliche Antikensammlung (State Collection of Antiquities) has a priceless collection of ancient vases, jewellery, bronzes and terracotta sculptures.

THE BASICS

www.antike-am-koenigsplatz.mwn.de

✚ H6

✉ Königsplatz

☎ Glyptothek 28 61 00. Antikensammlung 5998 8830

🕐 Glyptothek Tue–Sun 10–5 (Thu until 8). Staatliche Antikensammlung Tue, Thu–Sun 10–5, Wed 10–8

🍴 Glyptothek museum café

Ⓤ U-Bahn Königsplatz

♿ Good (Glyptothek); none (Antikensammlung)

💶 Moderate

Lenbachhaus

Lenbachhaus is a Florentine Renaissance-style villa

THE BASICS

www.lenbachhaus.de

✚ H6

✉ Luisenstrasse 33

☎ 2333 2000

🕐 Tue–Sun 10–6

🍴 Café and garden terrace

Ⓤ U-Bahn Königsplatz

♿ Good

💶 Moderate

❓ *Der Blaue Reiter* guided tours Sun 11am (organized by the Munich Volkshochschule)

HIGHLIGHTS

● Kandinsky collection
● *Der Blaue Reiter* collection
● *Show your Wounds*, Joseph Beuys
● *Blue Horse*, Franz Marc
● Munich Jugendstil collection

This beautiful city gallery displays predominantly 19th- and 20th-century works of art. The tiny formal garden is also a delight—a blend of modern and classical statuary and fountains.

The Lenbachhaus This charming villa was built in 1887 in Florentine High Renaissance style by Gabriel von Seidl for the 'painter prince' Franz von Lenbach, darling of the German aristocracy and the most fashionable Bavarian painter of his day. After his death, it became the property of the city and was converted into the municipal art gallery (Städtische Galerie im Lenbachhaus). A north wing was added in the late 1920s to balance the south wing, where Lenbach's studio was housed. The resulting structure perfectly frames the terrace and ornamental gardens.

The collections The chief objective of the gallery is to document the development of painting in Munich from the late Gothic period up to the present day. Munich Romantics and landscape artists are well represented, as is the Jugendstil period. However, it is the paintings by the Munich-based expressionist group known as *Der Blaue Reiter* (Blue Rider) that gained the Lenbachhaus international fame. They include over 300 works by Wassily Kandinsky, who founded the movement with Franz Marc. Paul Klee, Gabriele Münter, August Macke and Alexej von Jawlensky are well represented, and the collection of contemporary art by Anselm Kiefer, Andy Warhol, Roy Lichtenstein, Joseph Beuys and others is dazzling.

The New Picture Gallery was designed by Alexander von Branca

Neue Pinakothek

The New Picture Gallery is a shining contrast to the Renaissance-style Old Picture Gallery across the road and carries the art collections on through the 19th and early 20th centuries.

Palazzo Branca As with the Old Picture Gallery (Alte Pinakothek), it was Ludwig I who instigated the building of this gallery as a home for contemporary art in 1846. However, following extensive damage in World War II, a competition was held in 1966 to design a new gallery in the heart of Schwabing, Munich's trendy student quarter.

Successful design The winning entry, by Munich architect Alexander von Branca, opened in 1981. The concrete, granite and glass structure, sometimes known as the Palazzo Branca, integrates art deco and postmodernist designs with traditional features in an unusual figure-of-eight formation around two inner courtyards and terraced ponds.

Art treasures The Neue Pinakothek contains over 1,000 paintings, drawings and sculptures spanning a variety of periods from rococo to Jugendstil, focusing on the development of German art alongside English 19th-century landscapes and portraits, and French Impressionism. It is best to follow the 22 rooms in chronological order, from early Romantic works, then on through French and German late romanticism to French and German Impressionism.

THE BASICS

www.neue-pinakothek.de

H5

✉ Barer Strasse 29

☎ 2380 5195

🕐 Wed 10–8. Thu–Mon 10–6

🍴 Café with terrace

🚇 U-Bahn Theresienstrasse

🚊 Tram 27

♿ Very good

💶 Moderate

HIGHLIGHTS

● *Ostende*, William Turner
● *Breakfast*, Edouard Manet
● *Vase with Sunflowers* and *View of Arles*, Vincent van Gogh
● *Large Reclining Woman*, Henry Moore

Pinakothek der Moderne

HIGHLIGHTS

- *World Peace Projected*, Bruce Nauman
- *Madame Soler*, Pablo Picasso
- *The End of the 20th Century*, Joseph Beuys
- *The Starting Line*, with installations by Metzel, Grimonprez, Rist, Dijkstra, Bock and others
- The *Entartete Kunst* ('Degenerate Art') collection
- Bauhaus furniture
- Bent wood furniture
- Mobile phone collection

With four major museums under one roof, the Pinakothek der Moderne, founded in 2002, is regarded as one of the world's greatest collections of 20th- and 21st-century art.

State Gallery of Modern Art Half of the total exhibition space in the Pinakothek is occupied by modern art, with an exceptional display of paintings, sculptures, video installations and photographic art, plus incomparable collections of German expressionism and surrealism. Works by Magritte, Picasso, Dalí and Warhol characterize 20th-century art movements, while more recent trends are represented by Rist, Falvin and Wall.

The New Collection This is one of the leading international collections of applied modern arts—a

Private sponsors helped to save the Pinakothek der Moderne when the state ran out of money during its construction. It is now the largest museum structure in Europe

veritable treasure trove of more than 50,000 items (arranged chronologically) illustrating the history of design, with exhibits ranging from cars to computers and from robots to running shoes. Highlights include the avant-garde of the 1920s and 1930s, functionalism, Pop-Art design and the space euphoria of the 1960s.

Architecture Museum The largest collection of its kind in Germany, comprising drawings, photographs and models of more than 700 international architects, displayed in temporary exhibitions examining current trends in German architecture.

State Graphic Art Collection Alongside the Architecture Museum are selections from the State Graphics Collection, which has over 4,000,000 etchings and drawings spanning seven centuries.

THE BASICS

www.pinakothek-der-moderne.de
✚ H6
✉ Barer Strasse 40
☎ 2380 5360
🕐 Tue 10–8, Wed–Sun 10–6
🍴 Café-bistro
🚇 U-Bahn Königsplatz or Theresienstrasse
🚌 100; tram 27
♿ Very good
👆 Expensive
❓ Free guided tours

More to See

HOCHSCHULE FÜR MUSIK
www.musikhochschule-muenchen.de
The music academy (formerly Hitler's 'Temple of Honour') was designed on Hitler's instruction by Paul Ludwig Troost.
➕ H6 ✉ Arcisstrasse 12 ☎ 2 89 03 🚇 U-Bahn Königsplatz

JUGENDSTILHAUS AINMILLERSTRASSE
Munich's first Jugendstil (art nouveau) house (1900) has been restored to its original glory.
➕ J4 ✉ Ainmillerstrasse 22 🚇 U-Bahn Giselastrasse

LEOPOLDSTRASSE
The 19th-century Siegestor (a triumphal arch topped with a chariot containing the figure of Bavaria) marks the beginning of the Schwabing district and this fashionable, poplar-lined boulevard. Here you'll find an array of street cafés, fashion boutiques and the wacky *Walking Man* (1995) sculpture by American sculptor Jonathan Borofsky, which is five floors tall.

➕ J5 ✉ Leopoldstrasse 🚇 U-Bahn Giselastrasse

LUDWIGSTRASSE
This grand avenue, which continues into Leopoldstrasse, was laid out by Ludwig I. It contains Peter Cornelius's *Last Judgement*, the second largest fresco in the world (after Michaelangelo's *Last Judgement* in the Sistine Chapel, Rome), which took four years to complete.
➕ J5 ✉ Ludwigstrasse 🚇 U-Bahn Odeonsplatz, Universität

MUSEUM BRANDHORST
www.museum-brandhorst.de
This new museum (due to open in 2008) will house the Brandhorst Collection, devoted to art in the second half of the 20th century. Highlights include the near-complete collection of illustrated books by Picasso and important works by Polke, Beuys, Nauman, Warhol and Hirst.
➕ J6 ✉ Theresienstrasse 35a ☎ 2380 5104 🚇 U-Bahn Königsplatz, Theresienstrasse 🚌 100; tram 27

Walking Man *on Leopoldstrasse*

Jugendstilhaus

Galleries and Gardens

From the world-class art galleries via Schwabing's trendy bars and boutiques to the Englischer Garten, this walk appeals to everyone.

DISTANCE: 1.8km (1.1 miles) **ALLOW:** 2.5 hours (excluding visits)

START

KÖNIGSPLATZ (▷ 66)
H6 Königsplatz

END

ENGLISCHER GARTEN (▷ 64–65)
L4 Münchner Freiheit

❶ Start at the grand and spacious Königsplatz (▷ 66–67), dubbed the 'Athens-on-the-Isar' for its grand classical-style architecture.

❽ While away the hours in the English Garden, then head northwards to the boating lake and neighbouring Seehaus beer garden (▷ 78).

❷ Here you will find yourself surrounded by museums: choose from the gallery in Lenbachhaus (▷ 68), the Glyptothek (▷ 67) and the Staatliche Antikensammlung (▷ 67).

❼ The university is marked by two fountains. A right turn here will lead you along Veterinärstrasse and into the city's vast green space, the Englischer Garten (▷ 64–65). The Chinese Tower nearby is the site of Munich's most popular beer garden.

❸ Proceed along Briennerstrasse, and turn left into Barer Strasse at the obelisk in Karolinenplatz. This is the heart of the city's 'Kunstareal' (art district), and the surrounding streets are brimming with small private galleries.

❻ The end of Schellingstrasse is marked by the Ludwigskirche, which contains one of the world's largest frescoes. Turn left here into Ludwigstrasse (▷ 72), a grand avenue laid out by Ludwig I.

❹ Before long you will pass by three of its most important galleries: the Alte Pinakothek (▷ 62–63); Neue Pinakothek (▷ 69); and Pinakothek der Moderne (▷ 70–71).

❺ Continue up Barer Strasse then turn right along Schellingstrasse, just one of the maze of streets behind the university, bursting with student life.

Shopping

2-RAD
www.2rad-schwabing.de
This shop has everything a bicycle fanatic could possibly want.
➕ J4 ✉ Georgenstrasse 39 ☎ 217 6383 🚋 Tram 27

LE CHALET DU FROMAGE
One of Munich's best cheesemongers.
➕ J4 ✉ Stand 11, Elisabethplatz ☎ 271 2243 🕐 Closed Mon 🚋 Tram 27

CHINA'S WORLD
www.chinasworld.de
This specialist shop sells antique Rosenthal porcelain.
➕ J5 ✉ Kurfürstenstrasse 15 ☎ 2738 9900 🚇 U-Bahn Universität, Giselastrasse

ELISABETHMARKT
Schwabing's answer to the Viktualienmarkt, and with surprisingly few tourists.
➕ J4 ✉ Elisabethplatz 🚋 Tram 27

FLIP
www.flipmunich.de
Stocks an impressive range of name labels specialising in cool ready-to-wear fashion and footwear for both men and women.
➕ K4 ✉ Feilitzschstrasse 6 ☎ 3808 8659 🚇 U-Bahn Münchner Freiheit

HALLHUBER
www.hallhuber.de
Leading labels at reasonable prices; popular with young shoppers.
➕ K4 ✉ Leopoldstrasse 25 ☎ 34 37 11 🚇 U-Bahn Münchner Freiheit

KINDER-AMBIENTE
www.kinder-ambiente.de
Beautiful toys, fittings and furnishings to create the perfect children's bedroom.
➕ G5 ✉ Schleissheimerstrasse 73 ☎ 1433 0230 🚇 U-Bahn Josephsplatz

KREMER PIGMENTE
www.kremer-pigmente.com
A tiny shop opposite the Neue Pinakothek selling over 500 different shades for artists in every medium from oils to watercolours, together with paper and brushes.
➕ H6 ✉ Barerstrasse 46 ☎ 28 54 88 🚋 Tram 27

KUNST UND SPIEL
www.kunstundspiel.de
A magical shop full of sturdy, educational toys together with an extensive arts and craft section.

TOYS

Germany has been one of the world's leading toy manufacturers since the Middle Ages, and is particularly famous for its china dolls, tin-plate toys and Steiff teddy bears. Many important manufacturing areas are around Munich–Nuremberg, Oberammergau and Berchtesgaden. Today, old Steiff bears are considered great collector's pieces.

➕ K4 ✉ Leopoldstrasse 48 ☎ 381 6270 🚇 U-Bahn Giselastrasse

LANDPARTIE
A warm country atmosphere welcomes you into this homely shop, crammed with antique furniture and household accessories.
➕ J5 ✉ Kurfürstenstrasse 10-12 ☎ 34 85 98 🚋 Tram 27

PERLENMARKT
www.perlenmarkt.de
This unusual shop sells nothing but buttons, beads and jewellery-making equipment.
➕ J5 ✉ Nordendstrasse 28 ☎ 271 0576 🚋 Tram 27

DIE PUPPENSTUBE
Dolls and puppets to take you back to your childhood.
➕ H5 ✉ Luisenstrasse 68 ☎ 272 3267 🚋 53

STOCKHAMMER
www.stockhammergeschenke.de
Idea-hungry shoppers are sure to find original gifts here.
➕ J4 ✉ Hohenzollernstrasse 33 ☎ 34 15 77 🚇 U- or S-Bahn Münchner Freiheit

WORDS' WORTH
www.wordsworth.de
There is a large range of English books, a Pooh Corner for children and a National Trust shop.
➕ J5 ✉ Schellingstrasse 3 ☎ 280 9141 🚋 53

Entertainment and Nightlife

ALTE GALERIE
www.alte-galerie.de
A youthful dance club and bar, in a cellar that trades Schwabing chic for genuine atmosphere and an eclectic range of music.
✚ K5 ✉ Kaulbachstrasse 75 ☎ 34 98 87 ⓘ Daily from 8pm ⓜ U-Bahn Giselastrasse

ARRI KINO
www.arri-kino.de
One of Munich's main arthouse cinemas.
✚ J5 ✉ Türkenstrasse 91 ☎ 3889 9664 ⓜ U-Bahn Universität

HOCHSCHULE FÜR MUSIK
www.musikhochschule-muenchen.mhn.de
Young up-and-coming musicians from the Music Academy give regular free evening concerts and lunchtime recitals. Call for details.
✚ H6 ✉ Arcisstrasse 12 ☎ 28903 ⓜ U-Bahn Königsplatz

LACH- UND SCHIESS-GESELLSCHAFT
www.lachundschiess.de
Germany's most satirical revues are performed here.
✚ K4 ✉ Haimhauser-Ursulastrasse ☎ 39 19 97 ⓜ U-Bahn Münchner Freiheit

MARIONETTEN-THEATER KLEINES SPIEL
www.kleinesspiel.de
Puppet shows for adults, with a repertoire of productions by such writers

as Bertolt Brecht, Ludwig Thoma and Ben Jonson.
✚ H5 ✉ Neureutherstrasse 12 ☎ 272 3364 ⓜ Tram 27

MÜNCHNER SOMMERTHEATER
www.muenchner-sommertheater.de
Each July the Munich Summer Theatre presents a series of popular open-air performances in the Englischer Garten's amphitheatre.
✚ K5 ✉ Rümelinstrasse 8 ☎ 98 93 88 ⓜ U-Bahn Alte Heide 🚌 Bus 187

ROXY
www.roxymunich
A popular place to see and be seen. Great for people-watching.

BEER GARDENS

The Bavarian capital city's renowned beer gardens thrive from the first warm days of spring to the annual drinking climax of the *Oktoberfest* (▷ 92), when they are augmented by huge party tents erected on a city meadow (Theresienwiese, ▷ 88). Before electrical refrigeration was invented, brewers planted chestnut trees above their storage cellars to help keep supplies cool, then put out tables and benches in the shade to welcome drinkers. To this day, the spring-flowering of the chestnut trees heralds the start of the beer garden season.

✚ K4 ✉ Leopoldstrasse 48 ☎ 34 92 92 ⓘ 8am–3am ⓜ U-Bahn Gisalastrasse

SCHWABINGER PODIUM
www.schwabinger-podium.com
A small, popular venue that does rock'n'roll and blues.
✚ K4 ✉ Wagnerstrasse 1 ☎ 39 94 82 ⓘ Mon–Fri 8pm–1am, Sat–Sun 8pm–3am ⓜ U-Bahn Münchner Freiheit

SKYLINE
www.skyline-club.de
New York-style bar and dance club with breathtaking views.
✚ K4 ✉ Leopoldstrasse 82 ☎ 33 31 31 ⓘ Daily 6..30pm–4am ⓜ U-Bahn Freiheit

THEATER BEI HEPPEL & ETTLICH
www.heppel-ettlich.de
A relaxed atmosphere and a glass of beer welcomes you to this student bar-cum-theatre.
✚ J4 ✉ Kaiserstrasse 67 ☎ 34 93 59 🚌 Tram 12, 27

THEATER DER JUGEND
www.schauburg.net
Shows here appeal to both small children (morning and afternoon performances) and teenagers (evening).
✚ J4 ✉ Schauburg, Franz-Joseph-Strasse 47 ☎ 2333 7171 ⓜ U-Bahn Giselastrasse

Restaurants

PRICES

Prices are approximate, based on a 3-course meal for one person.

€€€	over €50
€€	€25–€50
€	under €25

BACHMAIER HOFBRÄU (€)

www.bachmaier-hofbraeu.de
The menu at this comfy bar-restaurant goes beyond the expected Bavarian standbys, to take in a few continental dishes, and weekend brunch.
✚ K4 ✉ Leopoldstrasse 50
☎ 3838 680 ⏰ Mon–Thu 11am-1am, Fri 11am-3am, Sat 10am-3am, Sun 10am-1am
🚇 Giselastrasse

CAFÉ ALTSCHWABING (€)

www.cafe-altschwabing.de
Enjoy a leisurely breakfast in this elegant café with tasteful Jugendstil decor.
✚ H5 ✉ Schellingstrasse 56
☎ 273 1022 ⏰ Daily 9am–1am 🚌 53; tram 27

CAFÉ IGNAZ (€)

www.ignaz-cafe.de
One of Munich's few non-smoking cafés, serving some of the best vegetarian pizzas and risotto in town.
✚ H5 ✉ Georgenstrasse 67
☎ 271 6093 ⏰ Mon, Wed–Fri 8am–10pm, Tue 11–10, Sat, Sun 9am–10pm
🚇 U-Bahn Josephsplatz

CAFÉ PUCK (€)

www.cafepuck.de
A spacious, trendy student haunt in Schwabing. Excellent for breakfast.
✚ J5 ✉ Türkenstrasse 33
☎ 280 2280 ⏰ Daily 9am–1am 🚇 U-Bahn Universität

CAFÉ SCHWABING (€)

www.cafe-schwabing.de
Bavarian, French and Swiss breakfasts are the specialty of this café.
✚ J4 ✉ Belgradstrasse 1
☎ 308 8856 🚌 33; tram 12

SECOND BREAKFAST

With such a thriving café scene, taking breakfast in Munich is very popular. There are even a couple of home-delivery breakfast services in town. And, as many people in Munich start their working day very early, they often indulge in a mid-morning snack to bridge the gap between breakfast and lunch, called *Brotzeit* ('bread time'). This may be a sandwich or the traditional local specialty of boiled *Weisswürste* (white sausages) and *Brezen* (pretzels, knotted rolls sprinkled with coarse grains of salt). There are plenty of opportunities to indulge in *Brotzeit,* whether working in the office, eating on-the-move from a street stall or relaxing in a shady beer garden.

LE CÉZANNE (€€€)

This tiny bistro specializes in Provençal fare.
✚ J5 BKonradstrasse 1
☎ 39 18 05 ⏰ Tue–Sun evenings only 🚇 U-Bahn Giselastrasse

GRISSINI (€€)

www.grissini.com
An excellent Italian restaurant, decorated like an Italian palazzo.
AK3 BHelmtrudenstrasse 1
☎ 3610 1213 ⏰ Lunch, dinner; closed Sat lunch
🚇 U-Bahn Dietlindenstrasse

LENBACH (€€€)

www.lenbach.de
British designer Sir Terence Conran designed this restaurant, one of the most sophisticated in town, on the theme of the Seven Deadly Sins.
✚ H6 ✉ Ottostrasse 6
☎ 5491 300 ⏰ Lunch, dinner; closed Sun 🚇 U- or S-Bahn Karlsplatz

MAX EMANUEL BRÄUEREI (€)

www.max-emanuel-brauerei.de
Tiny, crowded beer garden, known for its folk music.
✚ J5 ✉ Adalbertstrasse 33
☎ 271 5158 ⏰ Daily 11–11 (evenings only in winter)
🚇 U-Bahn Universität

NEWS BAR (€)

www.newsbarmunich.de
Catch up on the news over breakfast with a selection of international newspapers and magazines.

➕ J5 ✉ Amalienstrasse 55
☎ 28 17 87 ⏰ Daily
7.30am–2am 🚇 U-Bahn
Universität

OSTERIA (€€€)

www.osteria.de
Top-notch Italian cuisine
in beautiful surroundings.
A venerable villa.
➕ H5 ✉ Schellingstrasse 62
☎ 272 0307 ⏰ Mon–Sat
lunch, dinner 🍽 53

PAPATAKIS (€€)

This Greek restaurant
is the place to be on
weekends if plate-
throwing and dancing on
the table is your scene.
➕ K4 ✉ Nikolaistrasse 9
☎ 34 13 05 ⏰ Daily dinner
only 🍽 33

ROSSO PIZZA (€)

Order a takeout pizza
here to enjoy in the
Englischer Garten, just a
two-minute walk away.
➕ J5 ✉ Amalienstrasse 45
☎ 2737 5653 ⏰ Mon–Sat
8am–10pm 🚇 U-Bahn
Universität

SAUSALITO'S (€€)

www.sausalitos.de
A fun, vibrant Tex-Mex
restaurant with a lively
party atmosphere and
sensational margarita
cocktails.
➕ J6 ✉ Türkenstrasse 50
☎ 28 15 94 ⏰ Sun–Thu
5pm–1am, Fri, Sat 5pm–3am
🚇 U-Bahn Universität

SEEHAUS IM ENGLISCHEN GARTEN (€€)

www.kuffler-gastronomie.de
Popular beer garden at

the heart of the English
Garden, overlooking the
boating lake.
➕ L4 ✉ Kleinhesselohe 3
☎ 38 16 130 ⏰ 10am–1am
🚇 U-Bahn Münchner Freiheit

SEOUL (€€)

Munich's only Korean
restaurant is in the heart
of Schwabing.
➕ K4 ✉ Leopoldstrasse 122
☎ 34 81 04 ⏰ Lunch,
dinner; closed 1st, 3rd Mon of
month 🚇 U-Bahn Münchner
Freiheit

LA STELLA (€€)

Terrific pizzas draw a
young crowd to this
excellent trattoria.
➕ I5 ✉ Hohenstaufenstrasse
2 ☎ 34 17 79 ⏰ Lunch,
dinner 🚇 U-Bahn
Giselastrasse

TANTRIS (€€€)

www.tantris.de
Munich's top restaurant,
with top chef Hans Haas
is renowned for its
excellent service and
contemporary cuisine.

VEGETARIAN SURPRISE

Think of Bavarian cuisine and
many people conjure up
images of enormous joints of
meat and miles of sausages.
However, Munich offers
some excellent vegetarian
restaurants. Their menus are
particularly interesting during
Spargelzeit (Asparagus
Season) in May and June
when asparagus is served in
an amazing variety of ways.

➕ K3 ✉ Johann-Fichte-
Strasse 7 ☎ 361 9590
⏰ Tue–Sat lunch, dinner
🚇 U-Bahn Dietlindenstrasse

TERRINE (€€€)

www.terrine.de
Exquisite Michelin star-
rated French food in a
smart art deco setting.
➕ J5 ✉ Amalienstrasse 89
☎ 28 17 80 ⏰ Tue–Fri
lunch, Mon–Sat dinner
🚇 U-Bahn Universität

TIRAMISU (€)

www.tiramisu-online.de
This tiny Italian bar serves
excellent antipasti and
has a daily changing
pasta menu.
➕ J4 ✉ Hohenzollernstrasse
124 ☎ 308 6008
⏰ Mon–Fri 11.30–10, Sat
11.30–5 🚇 U-Bahn
Hohenzollernplatz

TRESZNJEWSKI (€€)

www.tresznjewski.de
This trendy brasserie,
opposite the Neue
Pinakothek (▷ 69), is
packed from breakfast
until the early hours.
➕ H5 ✉ Theresienstrasse
72 ☎ 28 23 49 ⏰ Daily
8am–3am 🚋 Tram 27

VINI E PANINI (€)

Bread, wine and
delicious snacks from
different regions of Italy.
➕ J4 ✉ Nordendstrasse 45
☎ 272 1743 ⏰ Mon–Fri
10–6.30, Sat 8–2 🚋 Tram 27

There's plenty to see in Munich's western suburbs, from the high-tech world of BMW and the Olympiapark to Germany's finest baroque palace at Nymphenburg.

Sights	82–88
Walk	89
Shopping	90
Entertainment and Nightlife	91
Restaurants	92

Top 25 **TOP 25**

Olympiapark ▷ 82

Schloss Nymphenburg ▷ 84

BMW Museum ▷ 86

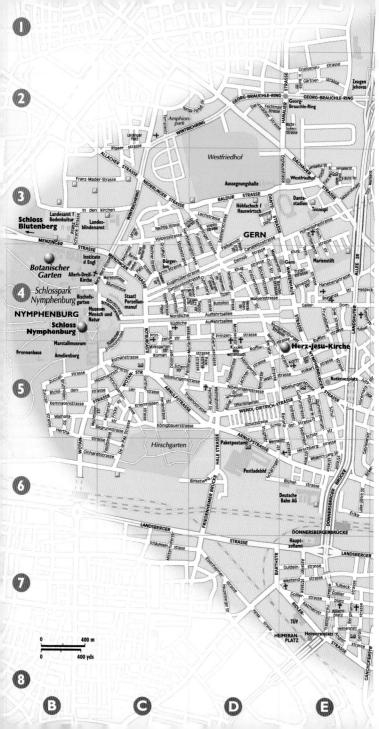

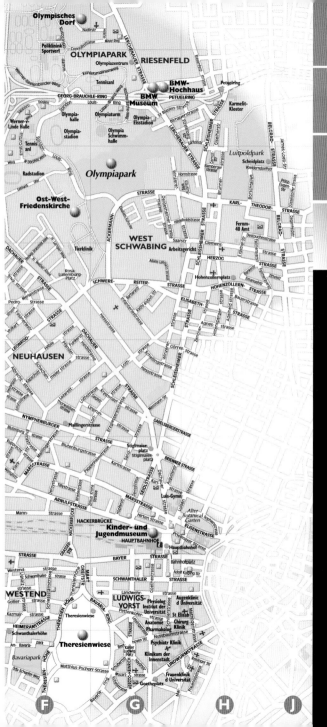

Olympiapark

Since the 1972 Olympics the park, with its intriguing skyline, has become one of the city's landmarks. Its tower offers an unforgettable view of Munich and the Alps.

The Games The historic Oberwiesenfeld was a former royal Bavarian parade ground north of the city. In 1909 the world's first airship landed here, and from 1925 until 1939 it was Munich's airport. Used as a dump during World War II, it was transformed in 1968 into a multifunctional sport and recreation area. In 1972 it was the site of the 20th Summer Olympic Games.

The buildings The television tower here, now called the Olympiaturm, built between 1965 and 1968, is the tallest reinforced concrete

Olympiapark was built for the Summer Olympics in 1972. The viewing platform of the Olympiaturm (Olympic Tower) at 190m (623ft) offers stunning panoramas

construction in Europe, and has become a symbol of modern Munich. When the weather is clear, the viewing platform and revolving restaurant give a breathtaking panorama of the Alps; the view of the city at night is magical. The stadium's futuristic tent-roof looks like an immense spider's web. When you tour the area on a little train you will see the Olympiasee, a huge artificial lake; the Olympiaberg, a 53m (174ft) hill con-structed from wartime rubble; the quaint Russian Orthodox chapel built by Father Timofej, a Russian recluse, beautifully decorated inside with thousands of pieces of silver paper (▷ 88); and the Olympic Village (▷ 87), remembered sadly today as the scene of the terrorist attack on 5 September 1972, in which 11 Israeli athletes and coaches and a German police officer were killed.

THE BASICS

www.olympiapark-muenchen.de

✚ G3

✉ Spiridon-Louis-Ring 21

☎ 30 67 0

🕐 Olympiaturm daily 9–midnight. Olympiastadion mid-Apr to mid-Oct daily 8.30–8.30, mid-Oct to mid-Apr daily 9–4.30

🍴 Revolving restaurant

🚇 U-Bahn Olympiazentrum

🚌 173, 177, 178; tram 20, 21

Schloss Nymphenburg

HIGHLIGHTS

- Amalienburg
- Badenburg
- Gallery of Beauties
- Porcelain Museum
- Magdalenenklause
- Marstallmuseum
- Botanical Garden (▷ 87)

TIPS

- On weekends, the gardens are especially popular.
- Be sure to visit the Badenburg, said to be Europe's first post-Roman heated pool.

It is hard to believe that one of Germany's largest baroque palaces, set in magnificent parkland, started life as a modest summer villa. This is one of Munich's loveliest areas.

The palace Five generations of Bavarian royalty were involved in the construction of this vast palace, starting with Elector Ferdinand Maria. Thrilled by the birth of his heir Max Emanuel, he had the central section built for his wife, Henriette Adelaide of Savoy, commissioning an Italian-style villa by Agostino Barelli in 1664. The villa was completed 10 years later. However, starting with Max Emanuel, each succeeding ruler added to the building, resulting in a majestic, semicircular construction, stretching 500m (550yds) from one wing to the other.

The beautiful Schloss Nymphenburg through the seasons

The interior The central structure contains sumptuous galleries, including Ludwig I's Gallery of Beauties, featuring 36 Munich ladies, some said to have been the king's mistresses. In the old stables, the Marstallmuseum's dazzling collection of state carriages and sleighs recalls the heyday of the Wittelsbach family. The Porcelain Museum provides a comprehensive history of the famous Nymphenburg porcelain factory (▷ 90) since its foundation in 1747.

Park and pavilions Originally in Italian then French baroque style, the gardens were transformed in 1803 into a fashionable English park with ornate waterways, statues, pavilions and a maze. See yourself reflected 10-fold in the Hall of Mirrors in the Amalienburg hunting lodge and visit the shell-encrusted Magdalenenklause hermitage.

THE BASICS

www.schloesser.bayern.de
✚ B4
☎ 17 90 80
🕐 Palace Apr–mid-Oct daily 9–6; mid-Oct–end Mar daily 10–4. Botanical Gardens May–end Aug daily 6am–7pm; Apr, Sep 9–6; Feb, Mar, Oct 9–5; Jan, Nov, Dec 9–4.30
🍴 Café Palmenhaus
Ⓤ U-Bahn Rotkreuzplatz
🚋 51; tram 12, 16, 17
♿ None
💶 Moderate

BMW Museum

THE BASICS

www.bmw-museum.de

G2

Am Olympiapark 2
(Petuelring)

01802 11 88 22

Tue–Fri 9–6, Sat and
Sun 10–8

U-Bahn
Olympiazentrum

36, 41, 43, 81, 136, 184

Excellent

Expensive

Phone in advance for a
factory tour

HIGHLIGHTS

● 1899 Wartburg Motor
Wagon
● 1923 R32 motorcycle
● 1931 Cabriolet
● 1934 Roadster
● 1936 BMW 328
● 1952 The 'Baroque Angel'
(BMW 501)
● 1955 BMW 507 roadster

Even if the world of automobiles doesn't particularly interest you, it's hard not to marvel at the developments of transport technology over the past five generations presented at the most popular company museum in Germany.

The museum The BMW Time Horizon Museum, housed in a silvery, windowless half sphere, provides an eye-catching contrast to the adjacent high-rise headquarters of the BMW headquarters (▷ 87). Over a quarter of a million visitors come to the BMW Museum annually to see its fascinating display of rare cars and motorcycles. As well as vintage BMW models, there are also insights into the past through slides and videos covering such subjects as changing family life and work conditions, the role of women in industry and car recycling (where BMW is at the forefront of development).

Future vision Take a simulated journey into the future with electric or solar-generated hydrogen-drive cars or design your own model and watch it develop on computers. Adults and children vie with each other to sit in the cockpit of tomorrow's car and experiment with its sophisticated data and information systems. At the museum's cinema, a film *Das weisse Phantom* ('The White Phantom') about motorcycle race world champion Ernst Jakob Henne brings the world of motor-racing to life. Just across Lerchenauer Strasse is the futuristic BMW Welt (World) building, where car buyers can take delivery direct from the factory.

More to See

BMW-HOCHAUS

This giant, silver, four-cylinder building resembles a four-leaf clover. The company's headquarters was built between 1970 and 1972 to a design by Viennese architect Karl Schwanzer to signal BMW's company's technical orientation.

✚ G2 ✉ Petuelring 130 🚇 U-Bahn Petuelring

BOTANISCHER GARTEN

www.botmuc.de

The Botanical Garden lies at the northern end of the Nymphenburger Park (▷ 84-85) and attracts visitors to its outdoor gardens and greenhouses over 20ha (50 acres). The best time to see the gardens in full bloom is in May and June.

✚ B4 ✉ Menzinger Strasse 65 ☎ 17861 🕐 Nov–Jan 9–4.30; Feb–Mar, Oct 9–5; Apr–Sep 9–6; May–end Aug daily 9–7 🍴 Café 🚌 Tram 17 💷 Inexpensive

HERZ-JESU-KIRCHE

www.herzjesu-muenchen.de

The 'Heart of Jesus Church' was completely rebuilt after a fire destroyed the old church in 1994. The new architectural wonder lays claim to the largest church doors in the world, while the façade is covered in glass panels. On the portal wings the Passion of Christ is depicted in a series of iconographical images.

✚ E5 ✉ Lachnerstrasse 8 ☎ 130 6750 🕐 Daily 8–8 🚇 U-Bahn Rotkreuzplatz 💷 Free

KINDER- UND JUGENDMUSEUM

www.kidimu.muc.kobis.de

There is a wide variety of hands-on activities and exhibitions that will delight children and young people in this museum, which aims to promote active learning and awaken curiosity.

✚ G6 ✉ Arnulfstrasse 3 ☎ 089 5454 0880 🕐 Tue–Fri 2–5.30, Sat, Sun 11–5.30 🚇 Hauptbahnhof 💷 Moderate

OLYMPISCHES DORF

During the Summer Olympics of 1972, athletes from around the world stayed in the apartments and

Botanischer Garten at the north end of the Nymphenburger Park

BMW Headquarters at night

bungalows here in the Olympic Village. Now most of them are privately owned or occupied by students.

🞩 F1 🚇 U-Bahn Olympiazentrum

OST-WEST-FRIEDENSKIRCHE

This unusual Russian Orthodox church was made from refuse, such as tin cans and sweet wrappers, by the Russian hermit Father Timofej, who lived here for decades before he died in 2004. When ordered to leave to make way for the Olympic riding stadium, he protested with the help of some Munich citizens and the stadium was constructed elsewhere.

🞩 F3 🚇 U-Bahn Olympiazentrum

SCHLOSS BLUTENBURG

A moated 15th-century castle in Obermenzing. The romantic Schloss Blutenberg was originally built as a love-nest for Agnes Bernauer by her secret lover, Duke Albrecht, III in 1438. Sadly, their romance never had a chance to flourish as, shortly after completion of the magical castle, she was accused of being a witch and was drowned in the Danube at Straubing. This one-time Wittelsbach summer residence contains an international collection of children's books—the largest library of youth literature in the world, with more than 500,000 books in 100 different languages.

🞩 Off map to west ✉ Seldweg 15, Obermenzing ☎ 17 90 80 🕐 Chapel daily Apr–end Sep 9–5; Oct–end Mar 10–4. Library Mon–Fri 2pm–6pm 🚇 S-Bahn Obermenzing 🎫 Free admission to chapel

THERESIENWIESE

'Theresa's fields' are best known as the venue for the world's biggest beer festival—the *Oktoberfest*, with its hefty beermaids serving the heaving throng. It all began in 1810 with the wedding party of Crown Prince Ludwig and Princess Theresa—a lavish affair with horse racing, shooting matches and a fair but, ironically, no beer. Here too is the 18m (60ft) high Statue of Bavaria; climb the 112 steps inside for great city views.

🞩 F8 ✉ Theresienwiese 🚇 U-Bahn Theresienwiese

Schloss Blutenburg

Oktoberfest at Theresienwiese

Green Munich

Escape the bustling city centre and visit Schloss Nymphenburg and its gardens, followed by a canal-side stroll to the Olympiapark.

DISTANCE: 3.5km (2.2 miles) **ALLOW:** all day (including visits)

START **END**

ROTKREUZPLATZ
✚ E5 ◎ U-Bahn Rotkreuzplatz

OLYMPIAPARK (▷ 82-83)
✚ G3 ◎ U-Bahn Olympiapark

❶ Start at Rotkreuzplatz, and head northwards up Nymphenburgerstrasse. After a short distance, turn left down Lachnerstrasse past the Herz-Jesu-Kirche (▷ 87).

❽ From here, it is a 2.5km (1.5 mile) walk through quiet, green suburbs, following the course of the canal all the way to the Olympiapark (▷ 82-83).

❷ Just past the church, turn right into Winthirstrasse. At the junction with Romanstrasse, note the ornamental Jugendstil (art nouveau) façade at No. 5 (to your right).

❼ Return to the canal via the Nordliche Schlossrondell, past the famous Porzellan-Manufaktur Nymphenburg. At Ludwig-Ferdinand-Brücke, turn left onto Menzingerstrasse. Cross the road and take a narrow right turn up Kuglmüllerstrasse immediately after the tiny Nymphenburg canal.

❸ Continue up Winthirstrasse past some of the grand mansions of this leafy, exclusive residential area until you reach the canal.

❻ The vast palace was constructed by five consecutive generations of Bavarian royalty, and contains several museums and galleries. The Porcelain Museum here provides a history of the famous porcelain factory (▷ 90).

❹ Turn left and stroll along the banks of the canal, along the Südliche Auffahrtsallee. During very cold winters, locals can be seen ice-skating on the canal.

❺ Eventually you will reach Schloss Nymphenburg (▷ 84-85).

Shopping

L'ANTIPASTO
www.lantipasto.de
A small, friendly Italian delicatessen selling mouth-watering antipasti, fresh pasta, sauces, wines and condiments.
🔲 F5 ✉ Mailingerstrasse 9 ☎ 18 49 79 🚇 U-Bahn Mailingerstrasse

ARMIN'S RÄUCHERKUCHL
A tiny, traditional Tirolean-style delicatessen, serving salamis, cold cuts and fine regional wines.
🔲 E5 ✉ Blutenburgstrasse 55 ☎ 12 92 123 🚇 U-Bahn Rotkreuzplatz

EILLES
www.eilles.de
This small, fragrant store specializes in fine teas, coffees, chocolates, biscuits and wine.
🔲 E5 ✉ Donnersberger-strasse 5 ☎ 16 15 35 🚇 U-Bahn Rotkreuzplatz

ESPRESSO & BARISTA
www.listino-prezzi.com
Espresso & Barista is an atmospheric café-cum-shop specializing in everything to do with coffee: cups, machines, drinking, even coffee courses.
🔲 E5 ✉ Schlörstrasse 11 ☎ 1678 38 8 🚇 U-Bahn Rotkreuzplatz

HUSSFELD ZANG
www.hussfeld-zang.de
Small but full of sophisticated gifts and stylish home accessories.
🔲 E5 ✉ Blutenburgstrasse

81 ☎ 1395 8421
🚇 U-Bahn Rotkreuzplatz

KARSTADT
www.karstadt.de
This branch of the Hertie department store chain stretches from the main train station to Karlsplatz and offers everyday items at reasonable prices.
🔲 H7 ✉ Bahnhofplatz ☎ 5 51 20 🚇 U- or S-Bahn Hauptbahnhof

KRISTINA SACK
www.kristina-sack.de
Fantastic kitchenware shop full of stylish tableware, quirky gifts and useful kitchen utensils. A must for all chefs!
🔲 E6 ✉ Wilderich-Lang-Strasse 6 ☎ 502 3464 🚋 Tram 16, 17

HANDCRAFTED PORCELAIN

The manufacture of exquisite porcelain figurines and dishes was started in 1747 by Prince Elector Maximilian III Joseph at his Nymphenburg Palace (▷ 84–85) in suburban Munich. Today about 85 artists and artisans keep alive traditional methods at a cramped factory across from the palace, throwing, forming and painting each piece by hand. Their delicate creations range from bowls and cups to graceful dancers and animals.

MOVE SPORTSHOES
www.moveshoes.de
From everyday sneakers to high-fashion trainers, this specialist store has the right style of sporting footwear for you.
🔲 E5 ✉ Nymphenburger-strasse 156a ☎ 167 5639 🚇 U-Bahn Rotkreuzplatz

OLYMPIA EINKAUFS-ZENTRUM (OEZ)
www.olympia-einkaufszen-trum.de
For everything under one roof, visit this huge shopping complex with over 100 shops near the Olympiapark.
🔲 E1 ✉ Hanauer Strasse 68 ☎ 1433 2910 🚇 U-Bahn Olympia Einkaufszentrum

PORZELLAN-MANUFAKTUR NYMPHENBURG
www.nymphenburg.com
This factory once created porcelain for the royal family and it still turns out beautifully handcrafted traditional designs. There is another outlet at Odeonsplatz (▷ 56).
🔲 C4 ✉ Nördliches Schlossrondell 8 ☎ 179 1970 🕐 Mon–Fri 10–5 🚋 Tram 17

WEIHNACHTSMARKT
A small, friendly Christmas market beside the Kaufhof department store at Rotkreuzplatz.
🔲 E5 ✉ Rotkreuzplatz 🚇 U-Bahn Rotkreuzplatz

Entertainment and Nightlife

BLADE NIGHT
www.muenchnerbladenight.de
Join tens of thousands of local roller-bladers touring the city on 'Blade Nights', every Monday night from May to September. Check website for times and routes.
➕ F6 ✉ Start in Wrede-strasse (near Hackerbrücke)
🚇 S-Bahn Hackerbrücke

CAFÉ AM BEETHOVENPLATZ
www.mariandl.com
Munich's oldest 'concert-café', combines the atmosphere of an old-style Viennese coffee house with a Bavarian-style beer garden.
➕ G8 ✉ Goethestrasse 51
☎ 552 9100 🕐 9am–1am
🚇 U-Bahn Goetheplatz 🚌 58

CAFÉ NEUHAUSEN
www.cafeneu.de
Mingle with the in-crowd at this stylish café with its long list of long drinks.
➕ F5 ✉ Blutenbergstrasse 106 ☎ 1897 5570
🕐 10am–1am 🚇 U-Bahn Rotkreuzplatz

CINEMA
www.cinema-muenchen.com
Probably the best cinema in town.
➕ G6 ✉ Nymphenburger-strasse 31 ☎ 55 52 55
🚇 U-Bahn Stiglmaierplatz

CIRCUS KRONE
www.circus-krone.de
Munich's internationally acclaimed circus offers shows from December to April.

➕ G6 ✉ Zirkus-Krone-Strasse 1-6 ☎ 5 45 80 00 🚇 S-Bahn Hackerbrücke

DAS SCHLOSS
www.dasschloss.com
Great theatre classics are performed all year round in a giant tent in the Olympiapark.
➕ G4 ✉ Schwere-Reiter-Strasse 15 ☎ 143 4080
🚋 Tram 1

DER REISEBÜRO
Reserve through this travel agent for one of Bavaria's most enjoyable experiences. On a *Gaudiflossenfahrt*, a pleasure raft trip on the River Isar from Wolfrats-hausen to Thalkirchen, you will drift downstream in a convoy to the music of a brass band and a steady flow of beer from the barrels on board.
➕ G7 ✉ Bahnhofplatz 2

OUTDOOR MUNICH

The Englischer Garten (English Garden ▷ 64-65) is a popular place for Munich's city dwellers to walk, cycle or sunbathe. This extensive green space stretches from the middle of the city along the banks of the River Isar. The Olympiapark (▷ 82-83), the stadium site of the 1972 Olympic Games, has been converted into a park with facilities including swim-ming, tennis and ice-skating.

☎ 55140-200 🚇 U- or S-Bahn Hauptbahnhof

MISTER B'S
www.misterbs.de
A small atmospheric jazz bar with daily live concerts at 10pm.
➕ G8 ✉ Herzog-Heinrich-Strasse 38 ☎ 53 49 01
🕐 Tue–Sun 8pm–3am
🚇 U-Bahn Goetheplatz

NACHTGALERIE
www.nachtgalerie.de
Former warehouse with plenty of dance space; popular for live bands.
➕ D7 ✉ Landsbergerstrasse 185 ☎ 3 45 55 952
🕐 Thu–Sat 10.30pm–4am
🚇 S-Bahn Donnersberger-brücke 🚋 Tram 18, 19

OLYMPIA-EISSTADION
www.olympiapark-muenchen.de
Try your hand at curling, a traditional Alpine sport, held on Thursday evenings at the Olympic Ice Stadium.
➕ G2 ✉ Olympia park
☎ 30 67-0 🚇 U-Bahn Olympiazentrum

OLYMPIA-EIS-SPORTZENTRUM
www.olympiapark-muenchen.de
Rent your ice skates at the door and enjoy this magnificent rink.
➕ G2 ✉ Olympiapark
☎ 30 67 21 50 🚇 U-Bahn Olympiazentrum

Restaurants

AUGUSTINER-KELLER (€)

www.augustinerkeller.de
One of Munich's most traditional beer cellars, just a few minutes' walk from the main station. Its popular beer garden seats over 5,000, making it one of the city's largest, after the Hirschgarten and the Chinesischer Turm.
🚇 G6 ✉ Arnulfstrasse 52
☎ 59 43 93
🕐 11.30am–1am 🚇 S-Bahn Hackerbrücke 🚋 Tram 16, 17

CAFÉ RUFFINI (€)

www.ruffini.de
The vegetarian menu served here is outstanding and the occasional meat dishes are equally good.
🚇 E4 ✉ Orffstrasse 22–24
☎ 16 11 60 🕐 Tue–Sun 10am–midnight 🚇 U-Bahn Rotkreuzplatz

HACKER-PSCHORR BRÄUHAUS (€–€€)

www.braeuhausanderbavaria.de
Ox-on-the-spit, the house specialty, is served to the accompaniment of traditional Bavarian music.
🚇 F7 ✉ Theresienhöhe 7
🕐 10am–midnight
🚇 U-Bahn Theresienwiese

HIRSCHGARTEN (€)

www.hirschgarten.de
Munich's largest beer garden, seating 8,500, is near Schloss Nymphenburg. Children love the deer enclosure and huge park.
🚇 C5 ✉ Hirschgarten 1
☎ 1799 9119 🕐 Daily 9am–midnight 🚋 Tram 17

KOSTBAR (€)

www.kostbar-muenchen.com
This popular 1970s-style café offers a hearty all-day breakfast menu.
🚇 G6 ✉ Augustenstrasse 7
☎ 5454 7799 🕐 Mon–Sat 8–1am, Sun 10–6 🚇 U- or S-Bahn Hauptbahnhof
🚋 Tram 20, 21

LÖWENBRÄUKELLER (€)

www.loewenbraeukeller.com
During the Lenten 'Strong Beer Season', men from all over Bavaria visit this beer cellar to pit their strength against each other in a stone-

lifting competition.
🚇 G6 ✉ Nymphenburger Strasse 2 ☎ 52 60 21
🕐 Daily 11am–midnight
🚇 U-Bahn Stiglmaierplatz
🚋 Tram 20, 21

SARCLETTI (€)

www.sarcletti.de
The largest ice-cream menu in town, with more than 100 flavours.
🚇 E5 ✉ Nymphenburger-strasse 155 ☎ 15 53 14
🚇 U-Bahn Rotkreuzplatz

SCHLOSSCAFÉ IM PALMENHAUS (€–€€)

www.palmenhaus.de
An elegant café in the Nymphenburg Palace's giant palm house.
🚇 B4 ✉ Schloss Nymphenburg ☎ 17 53 09
🕐 Apr–end Nov daily 10–6; Dec–end Mar daily 10–5
🚋 51; tram 12, 16, 17

TAXISGARTEN (€)

www.taxisgarten.de
This quiet, shady spot near the Nymphenburg Palace is renowned for its spare ribs.
🚇 E4 ✉ Taxisstrasse 12
☎ 15 68 27 🕐 Daily 10am–11pm 🚇 U-Bahn Gern

ZUR SCHWAIGE (€€)

www.zur-schwaige.de
Nourishing traditional fare in the south wing of Schloss Nymphenburg (▷ 84-85), or in the garden.
🚇 B4 ✉ Schloss Nymphenburg ☎ 1202 0890
🕐 Daily 11.30am–11pm
🚋 51; tram 12, 16, 17

There is even more to see outside of Munich's city centre. Bavaria has many attractions including several beautiful palaces, such as King Ludwig's fairy-tale castle, Neuschwanstein.

Sights   96–102

Excursions   103–106

Top 25   TOP 25

Bavaria Filmstadt ▷ 96
Dachau ▷ 98
Schleissheim ▷ 100

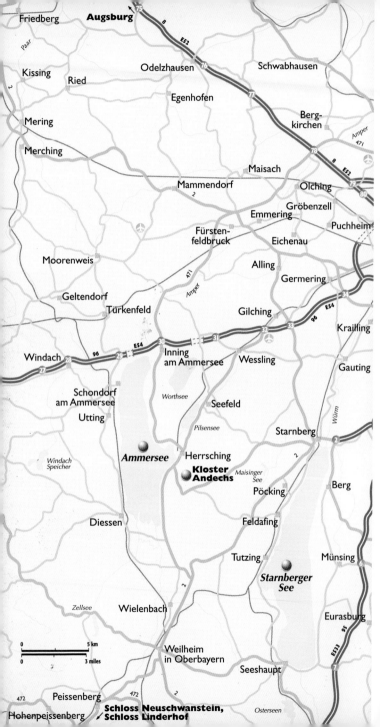

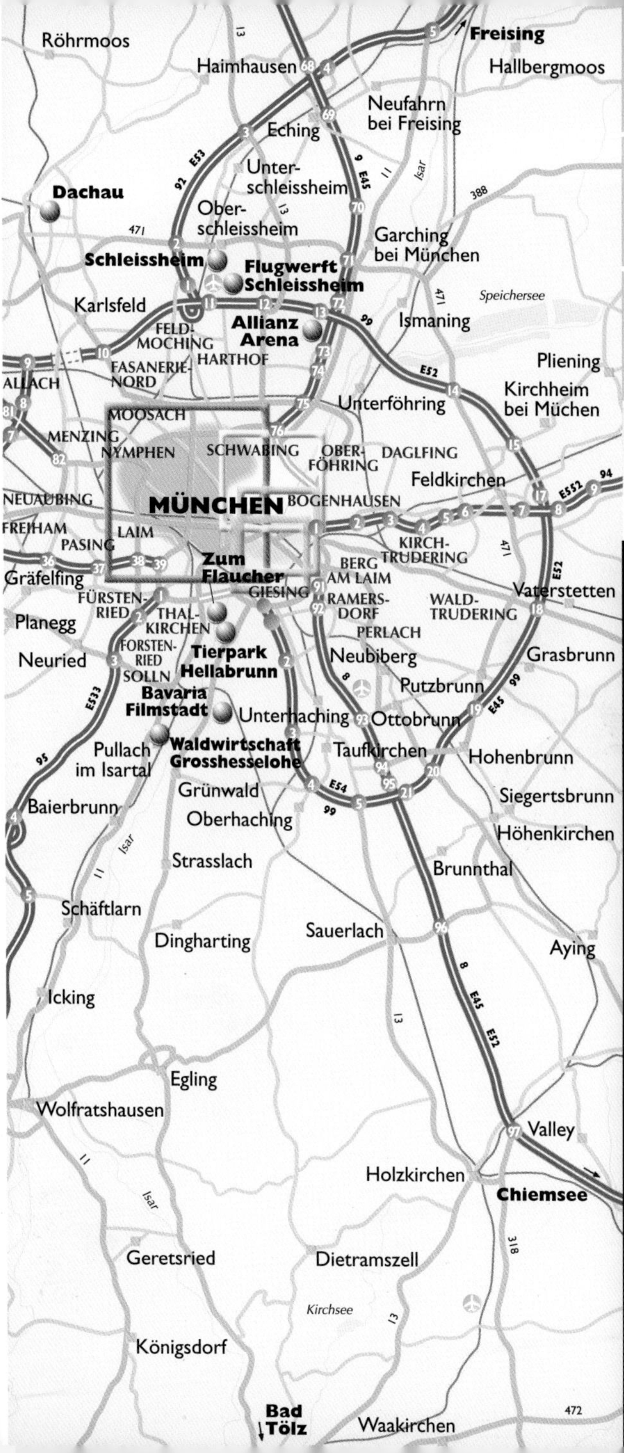

Röhrmoos
Haimhausen
Freising
Hallbergmoos
Eching
Neufahrn bei Freising
Unter-schleissheim
Ober-schleissheim
Dachau
Schleissheim
Flugwerft Schleissheim
Garching bei München
Karlsfeld
FELD-MOCHING
Allianz Arena
Ismaning
Speichersee
FASANERIE-NORD
HARTHOF
Pliening
ALLACH
Kirchheim bei München
MOOSACH
MENZING
NYMPHEN
SCHWABING
OBER-FÖHRING
DAGLFING
Unterföhring
NEUAUBING
MÜNCHEN
BOGENHAUSEN
Feldkirchen
FREIHAM
PASING
LAIM
KIRCH-TRUDERING
Gräfelfing
FÜRSTEN-RIED
Zum Flaucher
GIESING
BERG AM LAIM
RAMERS-DORF
WALD-TRUDERING
Vaterstetten
Planegg
THAL-KIRCHEN
PERLACH
Neuried
FORSTEN-RIED SOLLN
Tierpark Hellabrunn
Neubiberg
Grasbrunn
Bavaria Filmstadt
Putzbrunn
Pullach im Isartal
Waldwirtschaft Grosshesselohe
Unterhaching
Ottobrunn
Hohenbrunn
Baierbrunn
Grünwald
Taufkirchen
Siegertsbrunn
Oberhaching
Höhenkirchen
Strasslach
Brunnthal
Schäftlarn
Dingharting
Sauerlach
Aying
Icking
Egling
Wolfratshausen
Valley
Holzkirchen
Chiemsee
Geretsried
Dietramszell
Kirchsee
Königsdorf
Bad Tölz
Waakirchen

Farther Afield

Bavaria Filmstadt

HIGHLIGHTS

- Stunt show
- 4-D movie experience
- Model submarine for *Das Boot*

TIP

- Phone in advance to see if there is to be any TV recording during your visit, and request tickets to be part of the audience.

Glimpse behind the scenes of Europe's largest film studios, and learn the tricks of the trade. Since its renovation, Munich's 'Hollywood by the Isar' has more glitz and glamour than ever before.

Film Studios Founded in 1919, the Bavaria Film Studios has hosted major Hollywood productions as well as home-grown films. In the early 1970s, *Cabaret* was filmed here, starring Liza Minelli and Michael York, and directed by Bob Fosse.

Famous films In the 1980s, the studios became famous for Wolfgang Peterson's movies, such as *Das Boot*, *Enemy Mine* and *The Never Ending Story*. It was at this time that the Bavaria Film Tours began, and today you can still visit the fascinating sets for all three films.

At the Bavaria Stunt Show at these film studios you can learn how dangerous stunts are staged, while the film workshop allows school groups to shoot their own movie

Film tours Tours of the film studios last 90 minutes (with an English-language tour at 1pm daily). Older children will love directing their own films, and even playing the starring role in a thriller under coaching from one of the studio's directors. Explore familiar film sets (including an entire Berlin street, and the Gaulish village from *Asterix and Obelix versus Caesar*), watch actors at work filming local soap opera *Marienhof*, and be sure to see the breathtaking stuntmen in action in the Bavaria Stunt Show (which takes place on the set of a deserted New York suburb) with all its special effects and daring tricks. There is a thrilling 4-D motion cinema, where your seats move with the action in the film.

Munich also boasts more than its fair share of cinemas (over 84). Some show the films in their original language.

THE BASICS

www.filmstadt.de
✚ Off map to south
✉ Bavariafilmplatz 7
☎ 64 99 20 00
🕐 Mid-Mar to early Nov daily 9–5.30 (last admission 4pm); early Nov to mid-Mar daily 9–4.30pm
🚋 Tram 25
💲 Expensive
❓ Guided tours in English daily 1pm

Dachau

HIGHLIGHTS

● Schloss Dachau and Hofgarten
● Dachauer Art Gallery

TIP

● For a general overview, start your visit by watching a 22-minute documentary called 'The Dachau Concentration Camp', shown at 11.30am and 3.30pm in English, and at 11am and 3pm in German.

Once people visited Dachau to see the Renaissance chateau and town, until it became synonymous with the Nazi reign of terror. Today the concentration camp (KZ-Gedenkstätte) has been preserved as a memorial to those who died here.

Summer castle The pretty little town of Dachau, with its 18th-century pastel façades and quaint cobbled streets, is set on the steep bank of the River Amper. The Renaissance castle above the town was once a popular summer residence of the Munich royals. Only one wing of the original four survives; it contains a large banquet hall with one of the most exquisitely carved ceilings in Bavaria. Nearby is the Dachauer Moos, a heath area often wreathed in mists, with a delicate light that is loved by artists.

Although Dachau is home to a former concentration camp, it is also a lovely historic town that deserves to be explored in its own right

The camp Munich residents used to come to Dachau to wander its picturesque streets and visit the castle. But on 22 March 1933, only 50 days after Hitler came to power, Dachau was designated as the site of the first concentration camp of the Third Reich. Although it was not one of the main extermination camps, 31,951 deaths were recorded here between 1933 and 1945. Some original buildings have been restored as a memorial, a poignant reminder of the fate of the camp's 206,000 inmates. The museum documents the camp's history and the atrocities that happened here, with the help of polyglot audio guides. There are tours in English at 1.30 (Tuesday–Friday), and 12 and 1.30 (Saturday, Sunday) in summer; and 1.30 (Thursday, Saturday, Sunday) in winter. The gates still bear the bitterly ironic slogan '*Arbeit macht frei*' ('Work makes you free').

THE BASICS

✚ Off map to northwest
🚇 S-Bahn Dachau

The Concentration Camp
www.dachau.de
✉ Alte Römerstrasse 75
☎ (08131) 66 99 70
🕐 Tue–Sun 9–5
🚌 S-Bahn to Dachau, then bus 726 to KZ-Gedenkstätte Haupteingang or 724 to KZ-Gedenkstätte Parkplatz
♿ Excellent
✋ Free

Schleissheim

TOP 25

The Old Palace now houses collections from the Bavarian National Museum

THE BASICS

www.schloesser.bayern.de
🚹 Off map to north
☎ 315 8720
🕐 Apr–end Sep Tue–Sun 9–6; Oct–end Mar 10–4
🚇 S-Bahn Oberschleissheim
🚌 292
♿ None
💷 Old Palace: inexpensive; New/Lustheim: moderate; combined ticket: expensive

HIGHLIGHTS

Old Palace
● Religious folk art
New Palace
● Great Gallery
Palace Lustheim
● Meissen Porcelain Museum

The three Schleissheim palaces capture the splendour of Munich's past. Make sure you see the Great Gallery, the delightful French-style gardens and the magnificent display of Meissen porcelain.

Old Palace In 1597 Duke Wilhelm V bought a farm to the east of the Dachau moor as a retirement residence. His son, Prince Elector Maximilian I, later transformed it into an Italian-style Renaissance palace, and called it the Altes Schloss Schleissheim. Today it contains part of the Bavarian National Museum, including an unusual gallery devoted to international religious folk art.

New Palace The beautiful Neues Schloss, the 'Versailles of Munich', was commissioned by Prince Elector Max Emanuel II as a summer residence. The largest palace complex of its day, it demon-strated his wealth and power. Despite severe dam-age during World War II, the sumptuous rococo interior remains largely intact. The Great Gallery, over 60m (197ft) long, contains the Bavarian State Art Collection. One of the most remarkable collections of baroque paintings in Europe, it includes masterpieces by Rubens, Titian, Veronese and van Dyck.

Palace Lustheim Separated from the New Palace by formal gardens and encircled by a decorative canal, Palace Lustheim was planned as an island of happiness for Max Emanuel's bride Maria Antonia. It now houses Germany's largest collection of Meissen porcelain.

More to See

ALLIANZ ARENA

www.allianz-arena.de

Munich's stadium, home to both its Bundesliga football (soccer) clubs—FC Bayern München and TSV 1860. Opened in 2005, it has a capacity to seat 69,900 people. Its futuristic façade, comprising nearly 3,000 inflated translucent foil panels, has earned it the nicknames 'life belt' and 'rubber dinghy'. It changes colour, lighting up in red or blue, depending on which of the two home teams is playing.

➕ Off map to northeast ✉ Werner-Heisenberg-Allee 25 ☎ 20 05-0 🕐 Apr–Oct 10–7; Nov–Mar 10–6 ♿ Excellent 🚇 U-Bahn Fröttmaning

AMMERSEE

Ammersee, with its lake promenades, boat sheds and sandy beaches, is set in lush green countryside at the heart of Munich's lake district, easily reached by S-Bahn. Highlights include a trip on Bavaria's oldest paddle-steamer and Kloster Andechs (▷ 102). The lake also offers a curious, inexplicable phenomenon: a *Schaukelwelle* (rocking wave), which crosses Ammersee from north to south and back again like a giant pendulum every 24 minutes, the water rising and falling about 10cm (4in) against the shore.

➕ Off map to southwest 🚇 S-Bahn Herrsching

FLUGWERFT SCHLEISSHEIM

www.deutsches-museum.de

A must for plane buffs, this extension of the Deutsches Museum's aviation display is located on a disused airfield.

➕ Off map to north ✉ Effnerstrasse 18, Oberschleissheim ☎ 3 15 71 40 🕐 Daily 9–5 🚇 S-Bahn Oberschleissheim 🚌 292 💰 Moderate

FREISING

www.freising.de

On the left bank of the River Isar, 32km (20 miles) northeast of Munich, Freising was founded in the 8th century. Its hilltop Dom (cathedral) dates from the 12th century and has a lavish baroque interior from the 18th century.

➕ Off map to northeast 🚇 S-Bahn to Freising

The glowing 'rubber dinghy' of Allianz Arena

Sailing boats on the Ammersee

KLOSTER ANDECHS

www.andechs.de

One of Germany's most important pilgrimage destinations, famous worldwide for its centuries-old brewing tradition and its *Andechser Bock* beer.

➕ Off map to southwest ✉ Bergstrasse 2, Andechs ☎ 01852 3760 🕐 The various elements of the complex have different opening times 🚉 S-Bahn Herrsching then by local bus 💰 Free

STARNBERGER SEE

Starnberger See is the largest of the five lakes just south of the city. The banks of the lake are still lined with the baroque palaces of Bavaria's aristocracy, and it remains predominantly the domain of the rich and famous. Today, the area offers many sporting activities—horseback-riding, golf, swimming and sailing.

➕ Off map to southwest 🚉 S-Bahn Tutzing (and earlier lakeside stations)

TIERPARK HELLABRUNN ZOO

www.tierpark-hellabrunn.de

The world's first 'Geo-Zoo' with animals grouped in habitats according to their regions of origin.

➕ Off map to south ✉ Tierparkstrasse 30 ☎ 62 50 80 🕐 Apr–end Sep daily 8–6; Oct–end Mar daily 9–5 🚉 U-Bahn Thalkirchen 🚌 52 💰 Expensive

WALDWIRTSCHAFT GROSSHESSELOHE

www.waldwirtschaft.de

A long-time local beer garden haunt overlooking the Isar gorge and famous for its live jazz.

➕ Off map to south ✉ Georg-Kalb-Strasse 3 ☎ 74 99 40 30 🕐 Daily 11–11 🚉 S-Bahn Grosshesselohe Isartalbahnhof

ZUM FLAUCHER

www.zum-flaucher.de

Somewhat off the tourist track, this scenic beer garden is next to the River Isar. Families bring their own picnics and candles here in the evening.

➕ Off map to south ✉ Isarauen 8 ☎ 723 2677 🕐 Daily 11–11 (restaurant open Sat–Sun 11–6 only in winter) 🚉 U-Bahn Brudermühlstrasse 🚌 54

Starnberger See, with the Alps in the background

Excursions

AUGSBURG

Bavaria's oldest city has a 2,000-year history and you'll find styles of all the major architectural periods. The Renaissance flourished here, and rococo became known as the Augsburg style.

Augsburg is Bavaria's third largest city, and its oldest, founded in 15BC as the Roman legionary fortress Augusta Vindelicorum. The city has many great buildings, monumental fountains and grand boulevards, as well as 15 museums and art galleries to visit. The Renaissance Rathaus dominates Rathausplatz; inside, the restored Goldener Saal (Golden Hall) is famous for its magnificent portals, ceiling and mural paintings. The Fuggerei (1514–23) are the oldest almshouses in the world. On Frauentorstrasse is Mozart House, the birthplace of Leopold Mozart, father of Wolfgang Amadeus, and now a Mozart museum.

THE BASICS

www.augsburg-tourismus.de
Distance: 72km (45miles)
Journey Time: 30–40 mins by train
🚆 Augsburg
ℹ Schiessgrabenstrasse 14, 86150 Augsburg
☎ 0821 502 0721

BAD TÖLZ

The beautiful spa town of Bad Tölz, at the foot of the Bavarian Alps, is famous for its iodine-rich springs and peat baths.

The elegant cobbled main street, lined with handsome pastel-coloured houses ornately decorated with murals, leads up to the twin-spired Kreuzkirche noted for its Leonhard chapel. Bad Tölz is a perfect base for skiing and other mountain activities. Nearby Blombergbahn is Germany's longest summer toboggan run and the scene in winter of a crazy sled-flying competition.

THE BASICS

www.badtoelz.de
Distance: 40km (25 miles)
Journey Time: 1 hour by train
🚆 Hourly trains from the main station
ℹ Max-Höfler-Platz 1, 83646 Bad Tölz
☎ 08041 78670

FARTHER AFIELD

EXCURSIONS

CHIEMSEE

Locally called the 'Bavarian Sea', Chiemsee is the largest of the Bavarian lakes. Its lush scenery and picture-postcard Alpine backdrop has attracted artists for centuries and today draws visitors to its shores for swimming, sailing and other pursuits.

The lake's main attraction is Herrenchiemsee, site of Ludwig II's ambitious summer palace—a replica of the French Palace of Versailles. Only the central wing of the building was completed, including the spectacular Hall of Mirrors. The smaller island of Frauenchiemsee has a fishing village and a Benedictine nunnery founded in 872, where the nuns still make a special liqueur, called *Klosterlikör*, from an ancient recipe.

THE BASICS

www.chiemsee.de
www.herren-chiemsee.de
Distance: 80km (50 miles)
Journey Time: 1 hour by train
🚆 Frequent trains to Prien from the main station
ℹ️ Chiemsee-Infocenter, Felden 10, 83233 Bernau am Chiemsee
☎ 08051 96 55 50 and (08051) 6090 (ferry)
🕐 Guided palace tours 9–6 (summer), 9.40–4 (winter)

SCHLOSS LINDERHOF

Set among magnificent mountain scenery and surrounded by forest, Ludwig II's Schloss Linderhof began as a hunting lodge belonging to his father, Maximilian II, and was based on the Petit Trianon at Versailles.

Completed in 1878, the lavish interiors, all decorated in Renaissance and baroque styles, include a hall of mirrors and an enormous chandelier weighing 500kg (1,000lb). Ludwig used the palace as a retreat and rarely received visitors here. The formal French gardens, fanciful fountains, grotto, Moorish kiosk and follies are a wonderful place to explore. The highlight—an exotic Moorish kiosk with a peacock throne—was acquired by Ludwig from the World Exhibition in Paris in 1876.

THE BASICS

www.linderhof.de
Distance: 100 km (62 miles)
Journey Time: 2.25 hours
🚆 Train to Oberammergau, then bus 9622
✉️ Linderhof 12, 82488 Ettal
☎ 08822 920349
🕐 Guided palace tours Apr–Sep 9–6, Oct–Mar 10–4
🖐 Moderate

THE BASICS

www.neuschwanstein.de
Distance: 120km
(75 miles)
Journey Time: About 2
hours by train
🚉 Füssen
☎ 08362 939880
⏱ Guided tours Apr–end
Sep daily 9–6; Oct–end Mar
daily
🚌 Daily excursions with
Panorama Tours
ℹ Tourist Information
Schwangau, Münchener
Strasse 2, 87645 Schwangau

SCHLOSS NEUSCHWANSTEIN

This fairy-tale castle is a magical white-turreted affair nestled in a pine forest in the foothills of the Bavarian Alps. In an attempt to make the fantasy world of Wagnerian opera a reality, 'Mad' King Ludwig commissioned a stage designer rather than an architect to design this romantic, theatrical castle, and watched it being built by telescope from his father's neighbouring castle of Hohenschwangau.

Neuschwanstein is the most photographed building in Germany, and the inspiration for Walt Disney's Sleeping Beauty Castle at Disneyland. Sadly only 15 of the 65 rooms were finished and Ludwig spent just a few days here before he was dethroned. The lavish interior is worth queuing up for, with its extravagant decor and vast wall paintings of Wagnerian scenes. Since childhood, Ludwig had a passion for German legend as epitomized in the operas of Richard Wagner. Following a performance of *Lohengrin*, Ludwig became an enthusiastic admirer and patron of Wagner, whose works inspired his eccentric building plans.

Together with Herrenchiemsee (▷ 105) and Linderhof (▷ 105), King Ludwig II's extravagant 'fairy-tale' castles were a drain on the regency's treasury. As state affairs became increasingly neglected, the doomed monarch was declared insane and, shortly after, met a mysterious watery death on the eastern shore of the Starnberger See (▷ 102).

Fortunately, Ludwig's request to destroy Neuschwanstein on his death was ignored. Just seven weeks after his death, the castle was opened to the public to pay off the enormous debts he had incurred building it. Today, the castle is the most popular and profitable tourist attraction in Bavaria.

Munich has its quota of luxury hotels, but it also offers authentic Bavarian accommodation, and some excellent youth hostels and camping options for those on a tight budget.

Where to Stay

Introduction   108

Budget Hotels   109

Mid-Range Hotels   110–111

Luxury Hotels   112

Introduction

There are more than 40,000 hotel beds in Munich. Budget accommodation is relatively easy to find; double rooms are better value than singles. If you are visiting in low season (November to March) you will probably be spoiled for choice–unless a large trade fair is taking place. The *Oktoberfest* (late September to early October) is a busy time, so you will need to reserve somewhere as much as a year in advance. The best advice is to reserve ahead whatever time of year you plan to visit.

Types of Hotels
Munich has its share of well-known hotel chains, but there are still many that are family-owned. Smaller, privately owned hotels sometimes do not have any rooms designated as non-smoking, so check when you book. Air-conditioning is not standard in Munich hotels, particularly those in historic buildings, and a few may not have an elevator. A large breakfast buffet is normally included in the price in mid-range hotels. Some smaller hotels and pensions do not accept credit cards. The Upper Bavarian countryside south of Munich is also geared to welcoming tourists, so you may consider staying there and commuting by S-Bahn, train or bus.

Star Ratings
Most hotels in Germany are assigned a star rating from one to five, and prices usually reflect this. However, bear in mind that higher prices are not necessarily a guarantee of quality. For this reason, it's always a good idea to ask to see a room before booking, or if you're making a reservation online, look at any pictures.

JUGENDHERBERGEN
The Germans are mad about hostels ('*Jugendherbergen*') and hostelling. Facilities are generally good, but some hostels require visitors to vacate the building during the day, and others have a curfew (although this is usually sensibly late). For reservations and further information, visit www.djh-ris.de, which has an English version.

Budget Hotels

A&O

www.aohostels.com
Low-price backpacker's hotel near the station and a popular budget base for the *Oktoberfest*.
🚩 H7 ✉ Bayerstrasse 75 ☎ 4523 5701 🚇 U- or S-Bahn Hauptbahnhof

ACANTHUS

www.acanthushotel.de
A generous breakfast served until late is provided, along with a phone, minibar and TV in the 36 rooms.
🚩 H8 ✉ An der Hauptfeuerwache 14 ☎ 231880 🚇 Sendlinger Tor

AM MARKT

www.hotel-am-markt.eu
A traditional hotel with 31 rooms, on one of the last original old squares near the Viktualienmarket.
🚩 J7 ✉ Heiliggeiststrasse 6 ☎ 22 50 14 🚇 U- or S-Bahn Marienplatz

BELLE BLUE

www.hotel-belleblue.com
This modern, minimalist pension is located near the main railway station and has 30 rooms.
🚩 G7 ✉ Schillerstrasse 21 ☎ 550 6260 🚇 U- or S-Bahn Hauptbahnhof

BLAUER BOCK

www.hotelblauerbock.de
A central hotel with 75 rooms and parking facilities. Great value.
🚩 J7 ✉ Sebastiansplatz 9 ☎ 23 17 80 🚇 U- or S-Bahn Marienplatz

BURG SCHWANECK

www.burgschwaneck.de
A long way out of the city, this youth hostel is in a castle overlooking the River Isar. Youth hostel pass required.
🚩 Off map to south ✉ Burgweg 10, Pullach ☎ 7448 6670 🚇 S-Bahn Pullach

EASY PALACE HOSTEL

www.easypalace.de
The clean and brightly furnished rooms at this invariably bustling modern hostel range from singles and doubles to 4- and 8- bed units. All are handily placed for the *Oktoberfest*.
🚩 G8 ✉ Mozartstrasse 4

CAMPING

For really cheap accommodation in Munich, why not bring a tent? There are three campsites in and around Munich. The best, and the most central, is Camping Thalkirchen (☎ 723 1707; www.camping-muenchen.de, attractively positioned along the River Isar, with 700 places open from mid-March until the end of October. There is no need to reserve except during the *Oktoberfest*.

☎ 55 87970 🚇 U-Bahn Goetheplatz

HAUS INTERNATIONAL

www.haus-international.de
Slightly more expensive than youth hostels, but you don't have to belong to a youth hostel organization to stay here.
🚩 H4 ✉ Elisabethstrasse 87 ☎ 12 00 60 🚇 U-Bahn Hohenzollernplatz

JUGENDHERBERGE MÜNCHEN (MUNICH YOUTH HOSTEL)

www.jugendherberge.de
Advance reservations and a youth hostel pass are essential here.
🚩 E5 ✉ Wendl-Dietrich-Strasse 20 ☎ 2024 4490 🚇 U-Bahn Rotkreuzplatz

MITWOHNBÖRSE– HOME COMPANY

www.muenchen.home company.de
Useful for longer stays, the Mitwohnzentrale will arrange apartment accommodation in Munich for a small fee.
🚩 K3 ✉ Germaniastrasse 20 ☎ 1 94 45 🚇 U-Bahn Dietlindenstrasse

STEFANIE

www.hotel-stefanie.de
A clean, friendly pension with 32 rooms in the popular university district a short distance from the three Pinakothek galleries.
🚩 J5 ✉ Türkenstrasse 35 ☎ 2 88 14 00 🚇 U-Bahn Universität

WHERE TO STAY BUDGET HOTELS

Mid-Range Hotels

ADMIRAL
www.hotel-admiral.de
This smart Hotel Garni with 33 rooms, near the river, offers special weekend packages.
➕ J8 ✉ Kohlstrasse 9
☎ 21 63 50 Ⓢ S-Bahn Isartor

ANNA
www.annahotel.de
A tasteful, modern hotel with 56 rooms, near to the main railway station, with underground parking facilities and young, helpful staff.
➕ H7 ✉ Schützenstrasse 1
☎ 59 99 40 Ⓤ U- or S-Bahn Hauptbahnhof

APOLLO
www.apollohotel.de
Rooms in this three-star hotel are quiet considering the location is so close to the Hauptbahnhof. About 25 rooms have a balcony. There is a little bar, which is open in the evenings.
➕ G7 ✉ Mittererstrasse 7
☎ 53 95 31 Ⓤ U- or S-Bahn Hauptbahnhof

CARLTON
www.carlton-garni.de
A hidden treasure for those in the know, this 49-room hotel, close to Odeonsplatz is reasonably priced.
➕ J6 ✉ Fürstenstrasse 12
☎ 28 20 61 Ⓤ U-Bahn Odeonsplatz

CORTIINA
www.cortiina.com
Smart, minimalist hotel frequented by a super-chic clientele. Internet portal in all 35 rooms.
➕ J7 ✉ Ledererstrasse 8
☎ 242 2490 Ⓤ U- or S-Bahn Marienplatz

COSMOPOLITAN
www.cosmopolitanhotel.de
Simple, modern hotel with 71 rooms. Surprisingly quiet considering it is in the heart of Schwabing.
➕ J4 ✉ Hohenzollernstrasse 5 ☎ 3 83 810 Ⓤ U-Bahn Giselastrasse, Münchner Freiheit

EXQUISIT
www.hotel-exquisit.com
A small, elegant hotel with a choice of 50 rooms, in a secluded side street near the site where the *Oktoberfest* takes place.

➕ H7 ✉ Pettenkoferstrasse 3 ☎ 551 9900 Ⓤ U-Bahn Sendlinger Tor

FLEMING'S CITY
www.flemings-hotels.com
This smart central 4-star hotel opened in 2006 and prides itself on its modern yet intimate atmosphere. Facilities include 99 stylish rooms, all with WLAN connections, a popular brasserie-cum-wine bar, and a small fitness area.
➕ H7 ✉ Bayerstrasse 47
☎ 4444 660 Ⓢ S-Bahn Karlsplatz (Stachus)

FLEMING'S SCHWABING
www.flemings-hotels.com
In the Schwabing area, this modern, 168-room hotel makes a good base for sightseeing and dining out. The hotel itself boasts a brasserie, wine bar, delicatessen and, in summer months, a beer terrace.
➕ K3 ✉ Leopoldstrasse 130–132 ☎ 206 0900
Ⓤ U-Bahn Dietlindenstrasse

GÄSTEHAUS ENGLISCHER GARTEN
www.hotelenglischergarten.de
An oasis on the edge of the English Garden; only 12 rooms in the main building and 13 in the annexe. Reserve well ahead.
➕ K4 ✉ Liebergesellstrasse 8 ☎ 383 9410 Ⓤ U-Bahn Münchner Freiheit

INSEL MÜHLE

www.weber-gastronomie.de
This beautifully renovated, timbered corn mill is one of the 'Romantik' chain of hotels and has 37 rooms. Just outside the city but worth the extra trip.

🔳 Off map to west 🖂 Von-Kahr-Strasse 87 ☎ 8 10 10 🚇 S-Bahn Allach

MARIANDL

www.hotelmariandl.de
A gem of a hotel just southwest of the city centre, the Mariandl has gracefully furnished rooms set in a turreted townhouse, and with the Café am Beethovenplatz (▷ 91) on the ground floor.

🔳 G8 🖂 Goethestrasse 51 ☎ 552 9100 🚇 U-Bahn Goetheplatz 🚌 58

PENSION SEIBEL

www.seibel-hotels-munich.de
This pension has bags of charm with traditional Bavarian decoration in the rooms and breakfast room. The location is great too–just behind the Viktualienmarkt (▷ 33). Book early for lower rates or stay in low season.

🔳 J8 🖂 Reichenbachstrasse 8 ☎ 2319 180 🚌 Tram 17, 18

SAVOY

www.savoy-garni.de
One of a small chain of hotels, together with the Carlton (▷ 110), offering simple, affordable accommodation in the heart of the city. It is ideally

located near the popular Leopoldstrasse shopping thoroughfare, and the Pinakothek art galleries.

🔳 J6 🖂 Amalienstrasse 25 ☎ 28 78 70 🚇 U-Bahn Odeonsplatz

SCHLICKER

www.hotel-schlicker.de
Good value hotel in a central location, near Marienplatz. The rooms overlooking busy Tal are double-glazed. Choose from doubles, triples, suites and a split-level maisonette.

🔳 J7 🖂 Tal 8 ☎ 242 8870 🚇 U- or S-Bahn Marienplatz

SEIBEL'S PARK

www.seibel-hotels-munich.de
This hotel is owned by the same family as Pension Seibel (▷ this page), but is not as central. Rooms are large with a radio, cable TV and telephone. There is also a sauna, to relax in after a hard day's sightseeing.

🔳 Off map to west 🖂 Maria-Eich-Strasse 32

PRICES

Like any metropolis, Munich can proudly claim a clutch of first-class hotels of worldwide reputation, but most of the city's 350-plus establishments are in the medium to lower price ranges. Except, that is, when a major trade fair or the *Oktoberfest* beer festival takes place, when prices can increase substantially.

☎ 829 9520 🚇 S-Bahn Pasing

SPLENDID-DOLLMANN

www.hotel-splendid-dollmann.de
A small, exclusive hotel in central Munich, with 37 rooms decorated in a range of styles including baroque, Louis XIV and Bavarian.

🔳 K7 🖂 Thierschstrasse 49 ☎ 23 80 80 🚇 U-Bahn Lehel

ST. PAUL

www.hotel-stpaul.de
Ideally situated for reaching the *Oktoberfest* ground, St. Paul has rooms with a safe, television, telephone and internet access. You can eat outside in the little courtyard in summer.

🔳 G7 🖂 St-Paul-Strasse 7 ☎ 5440 7800 🚇 U-Bahn Theresienwiese

TORBRÄU

www.torbraeu.de
This friendly, central hotel is the oldest in Munich, founded in 1490, and run by the same family for nearly 100 years. Its 91 rooms (some traditionally furnished; some more modern; all with WLAN) cater to families, individuals and business visitors. A café serves lunch until 2pm and cakes thereafter. The Italian restaurant offers room service in the evenings.

🔳 J7 🖂 Tal 41 ☎ 24 23 40 🚇 S-Bahn Isator

Luxury Hotels

PRICES

Expect to pay over €150 per night for a luxury hotel.

BAYERISCHER HOF
www.bayerischerhof.de
Classic, family-run hotel with excellent facilities including a roof-garden, health club, swimming pool and several top restaurants. 373 rooms.
H7 ⊠ Promenadeplatz 2–6 ☎ 2 12 00 🚇 U- or S-Bahn Marienplatz

EXCELSIOR
www.excelsior-hotel.de
In the tranquil pedestrian zone, three minutes' walk from the main station. 113 rooms.
H7 ⊠ Schützenstrasse 11 ☎ 55 13 70 🚇 U- or S-Bahn Hauptbahnhof

HILTON PARK
www.hilton.de
The Hilton has 479 rooms plus outdoor dining, beer garden, indoor pool, business area and views over the Englischer Garten.
K6 ⊠ Am Tucherpark 7 ☎ 38 450 🚌 54, 154; tram 17

KEMPINSKI HOTEL VIER JAHRESZEITEN
www.kempinski-vierjahreszeiten.com
Munich's flagship hotel, placed on the city's most exclusive shopping street, and within easy walking distance of most of the city's sights. 303 rooms.
J7 ⊠ Maximilianstrasse 17 ☎ 21 250 🚇 U-Bahn Odeonsplatz 🚊 Tram 19

KÖNIGSHOF
www.koenigshof-hotel.de
One of Munich's top hotels with 87 rooms and one of the best restaurants in town.
H7 ⊠ Karlsplatz 25 ☎ 55 13 60 🚇 U- or S-Bahn Karlsplatz

MANDARIN ORIENTAL
www.mandarinoriental.com
Guests at this 73-room, luxury hotel have included Prince Charles and Madonna.
J7 ⊠ Neuturmstrasse 1 ☎ 29 09 80 🚇 U- or S-Bahn Marienplatz

LE MERIDIEN
www.starwoodhotels.com
This chic, new hotel opposite the main station combines old-world charm with state-of-the-art amenities in its 381 sophisticated rooms and suites, together with a soothing spa to re-invigorate visitors.
H7 ⊠ Bayerstrasse 41 ☎ 24 22 0 🚇 U- or S-Bahn Hauptbahnhof

OPERA
www.hotel-opera.de
A small, plush hotel, with 25 rooms, set in a delightful old mansion with an inner courtyard.
K7 ⊠ St.-Anna-Strasse 10 ☎ 210 4 40 🚇 U-Bahn Lehel

PLATZL
www.platzl.de
A friendly hotel with 167 traditional rooms. Top-class facilities include a fitness area and a beautiful restaurant in a converted mill.
J7 ⊠ Sparkassenstrasse 10 ☎ 23 70 30 🚇 U- or S-Bahn Marienplatz

PRINZREGENT AM FRIEDENSENGEL
www.prinzregent.de
Tradition and comfort combine at this elegant hotel, with 65 rooms and an attractive garden.
L7 ⊠ Ismaninger Strasse 42–44 ☎ 41 60 50 🚇 U-Bahn Max-Weber-Platz

RITZI
www.hotelritzi.de
The aptly named Ritzi is central yet quiet, with 25 stylish rooms. It has a trendy bar and serves a great buffet breakfast.
L6 ⊠ Maria-Theresia Strasse 2a ☎ 4 19 50 30 🚇 U-Bahn Max-Weber-Platz

CRÈME DE LA CRÈME

The elegant, traditional Vier Jahreszeiten (Four Seasons) hotel was established in the mid-19th century as a guest-house for royalty visiting King Maximilian II and is still used today to accommodate visiting dignitaries. Its Vue Maximilian restaurant is well known for its superb cuisine (especially its Sunday brunch) and English afternoon tea is served in the lobby (▷ 58).

Everything you need to know to make your visit to Munich a success, from the initial planning stages through to practical tips on the ground to make your trip a memorable one.

Planning Ahead	114–115
Getting There	116–117
Getting Around	118–119
Essential Facts	120–121
Language	122–123
Timeline	124–125

Need to Know

Planning Ahead

When to Go

Munich is busiest between April and September when the weather is at its best. May is the start of the beer garden season while, in summer, the city is popular for its opera festival and lively park life. Autumn draws beer-lovers to the *Oktoberfest* (▷ 92) and December is crowded with shoppers who come for the Christmas market.

TIME

Munich is one hour ahead of the UK, six hours ahead of New York and nine hours ahead of Los Angeles.

AVERAGE DAILY MAXIMUM TEMPERATURES

JAN	FEB	MAR	APR	MAY	JUN	JUL	AUG	SEP	OCT	NOV	DEC
34°F	34°F	46°F	57°F	64°F	69°F	76°F	74°F	75°F	67°F	57°F	38°F
1°C	1°C	8°C	14°C	18°C	21°C	24°C	23°C	24°C	19°C	14°C	3°C

Spring (March to May) is at its most delightful in May, with mild days and the least rainfall.

Summer (June to August) is the sunniest season, with blue skies and long, hazy days, but also the occasional thunderstorm.

Autumn (September to November) is often still warm and sunny—the so-called *Altweibersommer* ('old wives summer').

Winter (December to February) is the coldest time of year, with frequent snowfalls.

WHAT'S ON

February *Fasching*: High-point of the carnival season, which begins in Nov.

March *Starkbierzeit*: Strong beer season.

April *Spring Festival*: A two-week mini *Oktoberfest* at the Theresienwiese.
Ballet Festival Week.
Auer Mai Dult: First of three annual fairs and flea markets.

May *May Day* (1 May): Traditional maypole dancing at the Viktualienmarkt.
Maibockzeit: A season of special strong lagers originating from North Germany.
Corpus Christi (second Thu after Whitsun): A magnificent Catholic procession dating back to 1343.

June *Spargelzeit*: Celebrates the many ways there are to serve asparagus.
Founding of Munich (14 Jun): From Marienplatz to Odeonsplatz the streets fill with music, street performances and refreshment stalls.
Film Festival: A week of international cinematic art.
Tollwood Festival: The Olympiapark hosts an alternative festival of rock, jazz, cabaret, food and folklore.

July *Opera Festival*: The climax of the cultural year.
Aver Jacobi Dult: The second annual Dult.
Kocherlball: A traditional workers' ball at 6am in the Englischer Garten.

August *Summer Festival*: Two weeks of fireworks and festivities in Olympiapark.

September *Oktoberfest*: The world's largest beer festival.

October *Aver Kirchweih Dult*: The third annual Dult.
German Art and Antiques Fair.

December *Christkindlmarkt*: Christmas market.

Munich Online

www.muenchen.de
The official Munich Tourist Office website, including online hotel reservations and general information on the local weather, city sights, guided tours, shopping, restaurants, nightlife and special events.

www.munichfound.de
The monthly English-language magazine *Munich Found* caters to visitors and residents alike with tips on local events, a comprehensive city guide and restaurant and nightlife listings, as well as children's sports and activities.

www.munich-partyguide.de
Up-to-date information on Munich's nightlife scene with details of all the latest bars and clubs. A must for party animals.

www.schloesser.bayern.de
A comprehensive and informative guide to the palaces, castles, fortresses, residences, parks, gardens and lakes in Munich and throughout Bavaria.

www.museen-in-bayern.de
Detailed site covering 50 museums in Munich alone, as well as in the surrounding region.

www.travelforkids.com/Funtodo/Germany/munich.htm
Brief descriptions of attractions for children and families in and around Munich.

www.mvv-muenchen.de/en
Everything you could wish to know about the Munich transport system, with maps, electronic timetables, tickets and prices for the city's S-Bahn (urban rail), U-Bahn (underground), trams and buses.

www.biergarten.com
A comprehensive guide (in German only) to the best of Munich's beer gardens.

GOOD TRAVEL SITES

www.munich-airport.de
For details of flight arrivals and departures, general travel information, airport facilities and transport links with the city.

www.fodors.com
A complete travel planning site. You can research prices and weather; book air tickets, cars and rooms; pose questions to fellow travellers and find links to other useful sites.

INTERNET CAFÉS

Coffee Fellows
www.coffee-fellows.de
✉ Leopoldstrasse 70
☎ 38 89 84 70
🕐 7am–midnight
🖱 €2.50 per hour

Cyberice
www.cyberice.de
✉ Feilitzschstrasse 15
☎ 3407 6955;
🕐 10am–1am
🖱 €1.50 for 30 mins; €2.50 per hour

Palmis Net Tuner Lounge
www.lounge.nettuner.de
✉ Occamstrasse 9
☎ 18 91 33 50;
🕐 Tue–Sun 11am–11pm
🖱 €2 per 1 hour

Getting There

ENTRY REQUIREMENTS

For the latest passport and visa information, check your relevant embassy website (Britain: www.britishembassy.gov.uk; USA: www.usembassy.gov)

TOURIST OFFICES

● **Hauptbahnhof**
✉ Bahnhofplatz 2
☎ 2339 6500
🕐 Apr–end Oct Mon–Sat 9–8, Sun 10–6; Nov–end Mar Mon–Sat 9.30–6.30, Sun 10–6
● **Head Office (administration only)**
Tourismusamt München
✉ Sendliger Strasse 1, 80331 München
🕐 Mon–Fri 10–8, Sat 10–4

● **Neues Rathaus**
✉ Marienplatz
🕐 Mon–Fri 10–8, Sat 10–4

German National Tourist Offices
● **UK** ✉ PO Box 2695, London W1A 3TN
☎ 020 7317 0908
● **US** ✉ 122 East 42nd Street, New York, NY 10168–0072
☎ (212) 661 7200
● **Australia** ✉ PO Box 1461, Sydney, NSW 2001
☎ 02 8296 0488
● **Canada** ✉ 480 University Avenue, Suite 1500, Toronto, Ontario M5G 1V2
☎ (416) 968 1685

AIRPORTS

Munich's international airport, Flughafen München Franz-Josef-Strauss, is located 28km (17.5 miles) north of the city, and offers services to over 150 destinations worldwide. Facilities include a bank, pharmacy and a medical facility, as well as a variety of shops, restaurants and cafés.

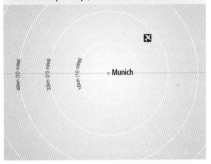

48km (30 miles)   32km (20 miles)   16km (10 miles)   ● Munich

ARRIVING AT FLUGHAFEN MÜNCHEN FRANZ-JOSEF-STRAUSS

For 24-hour flight information ☎ 97 52 13 13 www.munich-airport.de
The S-Bahn (urban train network) offers two services to the city from platforms located beneath the airport's main shopping area. S-Bahn 8 runs every 20 minutes from 4am until 1.02am, while S-Bahn 1 runs every 20 minutes from 5.50am until 12.10am, and also Monday to Friday at 4.30am and weekends at 5.30am. Buy tickets from the machines in the shopping area before going down to the platform. Remember to stamp your ticket in the blue punch-machine *(Entwerter)* on the platform to validate it before boarding the train. A single journey to the heart of the city costs €9.20. Alternatively, an airport bus leaves Munich North Terminal every 20 minutes from 6.20am to 9.40pm, taking 45 minutes to reach the main railway station. A single ticket costs €10.50.

ARRIVING BY BUS

There are frequent coach links with other German cities, starting from the main bus terminal beside the main railway station.

ARRIVING BY TRAIN

Trains take around 18 hours to Munich from Calais, in France, or Ostend, in Belgium. Munich has good connections with most major European cities. Most trains terminate at the main station (Hauptbahnhof). The east station (Ostbahnhof) takes regular motorail services from other German stations and from Paris, Budapest, Athens, Istanbul and Rimini. Train information from German Railways (Deutsche Bahn) is available in the main station's Travel Centre *(Reisezentrum)* ☎ 1308 1055.

ARRIVING BY CAR

Munich is well served by motorways (highways) and a ring road provides easy access to the city. Follow the clearly marked speed restrictions. Fines are harsh. Street parking is difficult in the heart of the city. Car parks charge around €18 a day. Try the Parkhaus am Stachus (Adolf-Kolping-Strasse 10) or the Parkgarage an der Opera (Max-Joseph-Platz 4).
• Car hire: Avis ☎ (01805) 217702

CONSULATES
• UK ✉ Möhlstrasse 5 ☎ 21 10 90
• US ✉ Königinstrasse 5 ☎ 28 880
• Canada ✉ Tal 29 ☎ 2 19 95 70

Getting Around

DISCOUNTS

● Children under six travel free and aged six to 14 at reduced fares.

● The City Tourcard, available from tourist offices, the main train station and some hotels. Unlimited travel for 24 hours on all public transport plus savings of up to 50 per cent on admission to major city attractions including museums, city tours, bicycle rentals and the zoo. The price ranges from €9.80 for a one-day card for one person, to €48 for a three-day family card.

VISITORS WITH DISABILITIES

Access for visitors with disabilities is generally good in Munich, although some older attractions and churches have few facilities. The Tourist Office's brochure *Munich for Physically Challenged Tourists* (in German) contains useful information on travel, lodgings, restaurants, arts and culture, city tours and leisure, and the MVV publishes a map detailing transport facilities.
For more information contact the Städtischer Beraterkreis Behinderte Geschäftsstelle (central advice bureau for people with disabilities)
✉ Burgstrasse 4 ☎ 2332 1178 or 23 32 11 79.

GETTING AROUND

U-Bahn (underground) and S-Bahn (suburban trains) provide a regular service within 40km (25 miles) of central Munich. Routes are referred to by their final stop. Underground trains run every 5 or 10 minutes from about 5am to 1am (later at weekends). Tickets are available from automatic ticket machines at stations, MVV sales points in many stations, or in newspaper shops. Before boarding a train, you must put your ticket in the blue punching machine *(Entwerter)*.

On buses and trams you must stamp your ticket upon boarding. Single tickets can be bought from the driver (with small change only). Multiple tickets, also valid for U- and S-Bahn, can be bought from vending machines at train stations, but not from the driver. Some trams have ticket vending machines on board. Bus and tram routes are numbered and the vehicle has a destination board showing where it is going. One late-night bus line Mon–Fri and six lines (Sat–Sun) and four tram lines operate between the heart of the city and the suburbs once an hour from 1.30am to 4.30am.

● Munich has an excellent, albeit complicated, public transport network, with two urban railways (S-Bahn rapid transit and U-Bahn subway), and a comprehensive network of bus and tram routes.
● The local transport authority is the Münchner Verkehrs- und Tarifverbund (MVV)
✉ Thierschstrasse 2 ☎ 4142 4344

TYPES OF TICKET
● The MVV network is divided into fare zones. Prices are based on the number of zones required to complete the trip. For most sightseeing you will remain in the *Innenraum* (interior area—marked blue on station maps). To travel farther you need a ticket valid for the *Gesamtnetz* (total network).
● Travelling without a valid ticket can result in a heavy fine.

• Kurzstrecke: short trip single tickets can be bought for journeys covering only four stops; two may be U- or S-Bahn stops. A trip must not last more than one hour and can only be used in one direction. Unlimited transfers are permitted.

• *Streifenkarte*: a strip of tickets. For each journey, stamp the appropriate number of strips. A 'short trip' is one strip. More than two U- or S-Bahn stops within one zone is two strips. If you are travelling outside the blue *Innenraum* zone, a notice shows how many strips you need to punch.

• *Einzelfahrkarte*: single tickets can be bought covering any number of zones, but a Streifenkarte usually works out cheaper.

• *Tageskarte*: one day's unlimited travel from 9am until 6am the following day. Purchase either a *Single-Tageskarte* for one person, or a *Partner-Tageskarte* for up to five people (maximum two adults).

• *Isarcard*: a weekly or monthly ticket providing unlimited travel on MVV transport, available at MVV ticket offices or ticket vending machines.

THE U- AND S-BAHN
• Smoking is banned on trains and in the stations.
• Bicycles may be taken on the trains all day Sat, Sun and public holidays; on weekdays not at rush hour (6–9am, 4–6pm).

TRAMS
• Scenic routes: trams 16, 17, 18, 19, 20, 21 and 27 operate around the old town; tram 20 goes to the Englischer Garten; tram 27 is useful for exploring Schwabing.

MAPS AND TIMETABLES
• MVV station ticket offices and tourist information offices supply free maps and information.

TAXIS
• Taxis are cream-coloured; stands are throughout the city. They are not particularly cheap.

WOMEN TRAVELLERS

• Frauenhaus München offers 24-hour help for women ☎ 35 48 30
• Some car parks have well-lit, reserved parking for women only near the main entrance ✉ Gasteig, Rosenheimerstrasse 5
🕐 6.30am–midnight
✉ Parkhaus Stachus Sonnenstrasse (entrance on Herzogspitalstrasse)
🕐 24 hours

STUDENT TRAVELLERS

• Some museums and theatres offer up to 50 per cent discounts with an International Student ID Card.
• A German Rail Youth Pass is available for young people under 26, valid for 4 or 10 days. Must be purchased outside Germany.
• For budget accommodation, camping and youth hostels (▷ 109).

Essential Facts

Toiletten are marked *Herren* (men) and *Damen* (women). *Besetzt* means occupied, *frei* means vacant. There is often a small charge.

The euro is the official currency of Germany. Bank notes are in denominations of 5, 10, 20, 50, 100, 200 and 500 euros and coins in denominations of 1, 2, 5, 10, 20 and 50 cents and 1 and 2 euros.

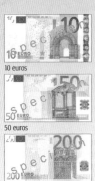

10 euros

50 euros

200 euros

500 euros

ELECTRICITY

● 230 (220–240) volts; two-pin sockets. Take an adaptor with you.

ETIQUETTE

● Say *Grüss Gott* (good day) and *Auf Wiedersehen* (goodbye) when shopping, *Guten Appetit* (enjoy your meal) when eating, *Entschuldigen Sie* (excuse me) in crowds.
● Never jump lights at pedestrian crossings. Don't walk on cycle paths.
● Dress is generally informal, except for at the theatre, opera or in nightclubs.
● Service is officially included in bills but tipping is customary.

MEDICAL TREATMENT

● A list of English-speaking doctors is available at the British and US consulates.
● Pack enough of any prescription medication you take regularly to last for the duration of your trip.
● Every neighbourhood has a 24-hour pharmacy *(Apotheke)*. Look for the address of that night's 24-hour *Apotheke* displayed in the pharmacy windows.
● International pharmacies have staff who speak different languages. Try Bahnhof-Apotheke ✉ Bahnhofplatz 2 ☎ 98 90 40 or Internationale Ludwigs-Apotheke ✉ Neuhauserstrasse 11 ☎ 55 05 070

NATIONAL HOLIDAYS

● 1 January, 6 January, Good Friday, Easter Sunday, Easter Monday, 1 May, Ascension Day, Whit Sunday and Whit Monday, Corpus Christi, 15 August, 3 October, 1 November, Day of Repentance and Prayer (during 3rd/4th week in November), Christmas Day, 26 December.

NEWSPAPERS AND MAGAZINES

● Bavaria's daily paper, *Süddeutsche Zeitung*, is published in Munich.
● Munich has several local dailies including the *Münchner Abendzeitung*, *tz* and *Bild-Zeitung*.

● An English-language listings magazine, *Munich Found*, is available from major newsagents.

OPENING HOURS

● Banks: Mon–Fri 8.30–3.45 (some open Thu to 5.30, many close for lunch).
● Shops: Mon–Fri 9–6, may change to 9–8 (late shopping Thu until 8.30), Sat 9–2, (but to 4 or 6pm on first Sat of the month). Many close for lunch (12–2).
● Museums and galleries: Tue–Sun 9 or 10am–5. Most close Mon and public holidays. Many are free on Sunday.

PLACES OF WORSHIP

● Roman Catholic: Frauenkirche, Peterskirche, Theatinerkirche and many others.
● Roman Catholic Services in English: Sunday at 10.30am in St John Kaulbachstrasse 33 and Sunday at 6pm in Kreuzkirche, Kreuzstrasse 2.
● Jewish: ✉ Reichenbachstrasse 27
● Muslim: Mosque ✉ Wallnerstrasse 1–3
● English services: International Baptist Church ✉ Holzstrasse 9; Sunday at 4pm Evangelical International Community Church ✉ Enhuberstrasse 10; Sunday at 11.30

POST OFFICES

● One of the largest post offices is opposite the railway station ✉ Bahnhofplatz 1 ☎ 01802 3333 🕐 Mon–Fri 8–6.30, Sat 9–4
● Most other post offices are open Mon–Fri 8–noon, 3–6.30pm, Sat 9–12.
● Post boxes are bright yellow and clearly marked 'Munich' and 'other places' *(Andere Orte)*.
● All letters to the UK and EU countries cost €0.70. The cost for airmail letters to the US and Canada is €1.70 for the first 5 grams, and €1 for postcards.

EMERGENCIES

● Police ☎ 110 ● Fire ☎ 112
● Ambulance ☎ 112 and 192 22
● Medical emergency service ☎ 01805 19 12 12
● Dental emergency service ☎ 723 3093/94
● Poisons emergency service ☎ 112
● Rape hotline ☎ 76 37 37
● Breakdown service ☎ 01802 22 22 22

LOST PROPERTY

● **Municipal lost property office:** ✉ Oetztalerstrasse 17 🕐 Mon–Thu 8–noon, (also Tue 2–6.30), Fri 7–noon ☎ 2 33 960 45
● For anything lost on the urban rail, underground, tram or bus contact MVV (☎ 4142 4344) for the transport company's number.
● For items left on Deutsche Bahn trains: **Fundbüro der Bundesbahn** ✉ Hauptbahnhof, opposite platform 26 🕐 Mon–Fri 6.30am–11.30pm, Sat 7.45am–11pm, Sun 7.45am–11.15pm ☎ 1308 6664

TELEPHONES

● Munich from abroad: dial 00 49, then the area code 89, followed by the number.
● From Munich: dial 00 and country code (UK 44, Ireland 353, US and Canada 1), then the number.

Language

There is one official standard German language, *Hochdeutsch* (High German), which everyone in the country should be able to understand. However, the regional Bavarian dialect, with a strong local accent, is widely spoken in Munich. The words and phrases that follow are High German.

BASICS	
ja	yes
nein	no
bitte	please
danke	thank you
bitte schön	you're welcome
Guten Tag/Grüss Gott	Hello
Guten Morgen	Good morning
Guten Abend	Good evening
Gute Nacht	Good night
Guf Wiedersehen	Goodbye
entschuldigen Sie bitte	excuse me please
sprechen Sie Englisch?	do you speak English?
ich verstehe nicht	I don't understand
Wiederholen Sie das, bitte	Please repeat that
Sprechen Sie langsamer bitte	Please speak more slowly
heute	today
gestern	yesterday
morgen	tomorrow
jetzt	now
gut	good
Ich heisse...	My name is...
Wie heissen Sie?	What's your name?
Ich komme aus...	I'm from...
Wie geht es Ihnen?	How are you?
Sehr gut, danke	Fine, thank you
Wie spät ist es?	What is the time?
wo	where
wann	when
warum	why
wer	who

USEFUL WORDS	
klein/gross	small/large
kalt/warm	cold/warm
rechts/links	right/left
geradeaus	straight on
nahe/weit	near/far
geschlosse/ offen	closed/ open

OUT AND ABOUT	
Wieviel kostet es?	how much does it cost?
teuer	expensive
billig	inexpensive
Wo sind die Toiletten?	Where are the toilets?
Wo ist die Bank?	Where's the bank?
der Bahnhof	station
der Flughafen	airport
das Postamt	post office
die Apotheke	chemist
die Polizei	police
das Krankenhaus	hospital
der Arzt	doctor
Hilfe	help
Haben Sie einen Stadtplan?	Do you have a city map?
Fahren Sie mich bitte zum/zur/nach...	Please take me to...
Ich möchte hier aussteigen	I'd like to get out here
Ich habe mich ver- laufen/verfahren	I am lost
Können Sie mir helfen?	Can you help me?

NUMBERS	
eins	1
zwei	2
drei	3
vier	4
fünf	5
sechs	6
sieben	7
acht	8
neun	9
zehn	10
elf	11
zwölf	12
dreizehn	13
zwanzig	20
einundzwanzig	21
dreissig	30
vierzig	40
fünfzig	50
sechszig	60
siebzig	70
achtzig	80
neunzig	90
hundert	100
tausend	1000
million	million

AT THE HOTEL/RESTAURANT	
die Speisekarte	menu
das Frühstück	breakfast
das Mittagessen	lunch
das Abendessen	dinner
der Weisswein	white wine
der Rotwein	red wine
das Bier	beer
das Brot	bread
die Milch	milk
der Zucker	sugar
das Wasser	water
die Rechnung	bill (check)
das Zimmer	room
Ich bin allergisch gegen..	I am allergic to...
Ich bin Vegetarier	I am a vegetarian

COLOURS	
schwarz	black
blau	blue
braun	brown
rot	red
grün	green
weiss	white
gelb	yellow
rosa	pink
orange	orange
grau	grey
lila	purple

Timeline

LUDIWG I, II AND III

Between 1825 and 1848 King Ludwig I transformed Munich into the Athens on the Isar, a flourishing hub of art and learning, and a university city.

In 1848 the king abdicated following political unrest and an affair with the dancer Lola Montez.

In 1886 Ludwig II was certified insane and later found mysteriously drowned in the Starnberger See.

King Ludwig III was deposed in 1918 in the Bavarian Revolution, led by Kurt Eisner, Bavaria's first Prime Minister.

(From left to right) Jugendstilhaus Ainmillerstrasse; Schloss Linderhof; Schloss Neuschwanstein; tapestry from Neuschwanstein; decoration from the Jugendstilhaus

777 First recorded mention of Munichen ('the home of the monks').

1158 Henry the Lion founds Munich.

1327 Munich suffers a devastating fire.

1328 Ludwig IV is made Holy Roman Emperor and Munich becomes temporarily the imperial capital.

1505 Munich becomes the capital of Bavaria.

1634 The plague reduces Munich's population by one third, to 9,000.

1806 Bavaria becomes a kingdom.

1810 A horse race celebrating the marriage of Crown Prince Ludwig starts the tradition of the *Oktoberfest*.

1864 Composer Richard Wagner moves to Munich.

1876 The first trams run in the city.

1900 Munich becomes a focus of the Jugendstil (art nouveau) movement.

1919 The assassination in Munich of Bavaria's first Prime Minister, Kurt Eisner, results in a communist republic.

1933 Hitler comes to power.

1939 World War II commences.

1940 First air attack on Munich (another 70 follow before 1945).

1945 American troops take Munich.

1946 Munich becomes the capital of the Free State of Bavaria.

1972 A terrorist attack ends the 20th Summer Olympic Games in tragedy.

1980 A bomb attack during the *Oktoberfest* claims 12 lives.

1990 The reunification of Germany.

1992 The World Economic Summit Meeting takes place in Munich. The new airport opens. Over 400,000 people participate in Germany's first *Lichterkette* (candle vigils) in Munich.

2003 Munich celebrates 350 years of opera.

2006 Opening ceremony and match of the soccer World Cup in Munich.

2008 Munich celebrates its 850th birthday, with events throughout the year.

RICHARD STRAUSS

Munich's greatest composer, Richard Strauss, was born in 1864, and eventually became the city's Kapell-meister (musical director). The breathtaking Bavarian scenery held a magnetic attraction for him, influencing his compositions considerably, and was particularly evident in his *Alpensinfonie*. His operas are still among the world's most popular and a fountain, depicting scenes from *Salome*, stands in the heart of the city as a memorial.

Index

A

accommodation 16, 107–112
airports 115, 116
Allianz Arena 17, 101
Alpines Museum 34
Alte Pinakothek 8, 62–63
Alter Hof 52
Ammersee 101
antiques 11, 12, 55
Archäologische
  Staatssammlung
  52
Architecture Museum 71
art district 73
Asamkirche 8, 16, 18, 26
Augsburg 103

B

Bad Tölz 103
banks 121
bars and clubs 13, 18, 40, 57,
  76, 91
Bavaria Filmstadt 8, 16, 96–97
Bavarian National Museum 9,
  46
Bavarian Observatory 34
Bavarian State Chancellery 53
Bayerische Volkssternwarte 34
Bayerisches Nationalmuseum 9,
  46
beer and breweries 4, 11, 17,
  47, 88, 92
beer gardens 15, 17, 65, 76
Bier- und Oktoberfestmuseum
  34
BMW-Hochhaus 17, 87
BMW Museum 9, 86
bookshops 11, 12, 38
Botanischer Garten 87
budget travel 16, 109
buses and trams 118, 119

C

cafés and bakeries 14, 15
camping 109
car hire 117
castles and palaces
  Residenz 8, 50–51
  Schleissheim 8, 100
  Schloss Blutenburg 88
  Schloss Linderhof 105
  Schloss Neuschwanstein 106
  Schloss Nymphenburg 8,
    84–85
Chiemsee 105
children's activities 16
children's shops 12, 39, 74
churches 18
  Asamkirche 8, 16, 18, 26
  Frauenkirche 9, 16, 18, 27
  Herz-Jesu-Kirche 17, 87
  Ludwigskirche 73
  Michaelskirche 18, 35
  Ost-West-Friedenskirche 88
  Peterskirche 8, 18, 31
  Theatinerkirche 16, 49

cinema 40, 76, 91
Circus Krone 16, 91
City Museum 9, 30
climate and seasons 5, 114
customs regulations 117
Cuvilliés-Theater 51, 57

D

Dachau 9, 98–99
Deutsches Jagd- und
  Fischereimuseum 34
Deutsches Museum 9, 24–25
Deutsches Theatermuseum 52
disabilities, visitors with 118
driving 117

E

eating out 13, 14–15, 16
  Bavarian cuisine 14, 15, 41
  Brotzeit ('bread time') 77
  brunch 18
  cafés and bakeries 14, 15
  mealtimes 14, 42
  vegetarian food 15, 78
  see also restaurants
electricity 120
embassies and consulates 117
emergencies 121
Englischer Garten 9, 16, 54,
  64–65, 91
entertainment and nightlife 13
  Innenstadt Nord 57
  Innenstadt Süd 40
  Maxvorstadt and Schwabing
    76
  West Munich 91
etiquette 14, 119, 120
excursions
  Augsburg 103
  Bad Tölz 103
  Chiemsee 105
  Schloss Linderhof 105
  Schloss Neuschwanstein 106

F

fashion shopping 10, 12, 38, 55,
  56, 74
festivals and events 114
Fish Fountain 28
Flugwerft Schleissheim 101
Föhn wind 5
food shopping 10, 12, 33, 39,
  55, 56, 74, 90
Frauenkirche 9, 16, 18, 27
Friedensengel 52

G

gifts and souvenirs 11, 12, 17
Glockenspiel 29
Glyptothek 67

H

Haus der Kunst 52–53
Herz-Jesu-Kirche 17, 87
history 124–125

Hitler, Adolf 4, 47, 52, 72, 99
Hochschule für Musik 72
Hofbräuhaus 9, 47
Hofgarten 49
hostels 108
hotels 108, 109–112

I

ice-skating 40, 91
Innenstadt Nord 43–58
  entertainment and nightlife
    57
  map 44–45
  restaurants 58
  shopping 55–56
  sights 46–53
  walk 54
Innenstadt Süd 20–42
  entertainment and nightlife
    40
  map 22–23
  restaurants 41–42
  shopping 38–39
  sights 24–35
  walk 37
insurance 117
internet cafés 115

J

Jugendstilhaus
  Ainmillerstrasse 72

K

Kinder- und Jugendmuseum 87
Kloster Andechs 102
Königsplatz 9, 66–67
Kunstareal 73

L

language 122–123
Lebkuchen 39, 58
Lenbachhaus 9, 68
Lenbachplatz 53
Leopoldstrasse 72
lost property 121
Ludwigskirche 73
Ludwigstrasse 72

M

Mann, Thomas 5
Marienplatz 9, 28–29
Mariensäule 34–35
Marionette Theatre Collection
  30
markets
  Christmas markets 39, 90
  food markets 12, 33, 39, 74
Marstallmuseum 85
Maximilianstrasse 16, 54
Maxvorstadt and Schwabing
  59–78
  entertainment and nightlife
    76
  map 60–61
  restaurants 77–78

shopping 74–75
sights 62–72
walk 73
medical treatment 120, 121
Michaelskirche 18, 35
money 120
Müller'sches Volksbad 35
Münchner Stadtmuseum 9, 30
Museum Brandhorst 72
museums and galleries
  Alpines Museum 34
  Alte Pinakothek 8, 62–63
  Archäologische
    Staatssammlung 52
  Architecture Museum 71
  Bayerisches Nationalmuseum
    9, 46
  Bier- und
  Oktoberfest museum 34
  BMW- Museum 9, 86
  Deutsches Jagd- und
    Fischereimuseum 34
  Deutsches Museum 9, 24–25
  Deutsches Theatermuseum
    52
  Flugwerft Schleissheim 101
  Glyptothek 67
  Haus der Kunst 52–53
  Kinder- und Jugendmuseum
    87
  Lenbachhaus 9, 68
  Marionette Theatre
    Collection 30
  Marstallmuseum 85
  Münchner Stadtmuseum 9,
    30
  Museum Brandhorst 72
  Museum Villa Stuck 53
  Neue Pinakothek 9, 69
  Photography and Film
    Museum 30
  Pinakothek der Moderne 8,
    70–71
  Porcelain Museum 85
  Schack-Galerie 53
  Spielzeugmuseum 8, 32
  Staatliche Antikensammlung
    67
  Staatliches Museum für
    Völkerkunde 53
musical events/venues 13, 17,
  40, 57, 76
Valentin Musäum 35

N
national costume 10, 39, 56
national holidays 120
Nationaltheater 9, 48, 57
Nazism 4, 47, 66–67
Neue Pinakothek 9, 69
Neues Rathaus 18, 28
newspapers and magazines
  120–121

O
Odeonsplatz 8, 49

Oktoberfest 88, 92, 108
Olympiapark 8, 17, 82–83, 91
Olympic Tower 16, 18, 82–83
Olympisches Dorf 87
opening hours 121
opera 40, 48, 57
Ost-West-Friedenskirche 88

P
parks and gardens
  Botanischer Garten 87
  Englischer Garten 9, 16, 54,
    64–65, 91
  Hofgarten 49
  Olympiapark 8, 17, 82–83, 91
  Schloss Nymphenburg 85
passports and visas 116
Peterskirche 8, 18, 31
pharmacies 120
Photography and Film Museum
  30
Pinakothek der Moderne 8,
  70–71
places of worship 121
police 121
porcelain 11, 56, 74, 90
Porcelain Museum 85
post offices 121
public transport 115, 118–119
puppet theatre 76

R
Residenz 8, 50–51
restaurants 15
  Innenstadt Nord 58
  Innenstadt Süd 41–42
  Maxvorstadt and Schwabing
    77–78
  West Munich 92
river trips 91
roller-blading 91

S
Schack-Galerie 53
Schleissheim 8, 100
Schloss Blutenburg 88
Schloss Linderhof 105
Schloss Neuschwanstein 106
Schloss Nymphenburg 8, 84–85
Sculpture Museum 67
Sendlinger Tor 35
shopping 10–12
  Innenstadt Nord 55–56
  Innenstadt Süd 38–39
  Maxvorstadt and Schwabing
    74–75
  opening hours 121
  West Munich 90
smoking etiquette 14, 119
Spielzeugmuseum 8, 32
Staatliche Antikensammlung 67
Staatskanzlei 53
Starnberger See 102
Strauss, Richard 125
student travellers 119
swimming pools 35, 91

T
taxis 119
telephones 121
Theatinerkirche 16, 49
theatre 13, 57, 76, 91
Theresienwiese 88
Tierpark Hellabrunn 102
time differences 114
tipping 120
toilets 120
tourist information 115, 116
Toy Museum 32
train travel 117, 118, 119
two-day itinerary 6–7

U
U-Bahn and S-Bahn 118, 119

V
Valentin Musäum 35
views of Munich 18
Viktualienmarkt 8, 33, 39
Villa Stuck 53

W
Waldwirtschaft
  Grosshesselohe 102
walks
  Galleries and Gardens 73
  Green Munich 89
  Munich's Old Town 37
  Royal Munich 54
websites 115
West Munich 79–92
  entertainment and nightlife
    91
  map 80–81
  restaurants 92
  shopping 90
  sights 82–88
  walk 89
  women travellers 119

Z
zoo 102
Zum Flaucher 102

Munich's
25 Best

WRITTEN BY Teresa Fisher
UODATED BY George McDonald
DESIGN WORK Jacqueline Bailey
COVER DESIGN Tigist Getachew
INDEXER Marie Lorimer
IMAGE RETOUCHING AND REPRO Michael Moody and Sarah Montgomery
EDITOR Jennie Liscombe
REVIEWING EDITOR Linda Cabasin
SERIES EDITOR Marie-Claire Jefferies

Fodor's is a registered trademark of Random House, Inc.
Published in the United Kingdom by AA Publishing

ISBN 978-1-4000-0380-8

FIFTH EDITION

IMPORTANT TIP
Time inevitably brings changes, so always confirm prices, travel facts, and other perishable information when it matters. Although Fodor's cannot accept responsibility for errors, you can use this guide in the confidence that we have taken every care to ensure its accuracy.

SPECIAL SALES
This book is available for special discounts for bulk purchases for sales promotions or premiums. Special editions, including personalized covers, excerpts of existing books, and corporate imprints, can be created in large quantities for special needs. For more information, write to Special Markets/Premium Sales, 1745 Broadway, MD 6–2, New York, NY 10019 or email specialmarkets@randomhouse.com.

Color separation by Keenes, Andover, UK
Printed and bound by Leo Paper Products, China
10 9 8 7 6 5 4 3 2 1

A03803
Maps in this title produced from mapping © MAIRDUMONT / Falk Verlag 2009
Transport map © Communicarta Ltd, UK

The Automobile Association would like to thank the following photographers, companies and picture libraries for their assistance in the preparation of this book.

Abbreviations for the picture credits are as follows: - (t) top; (b) bottom; (l) left; (r) right; (c) center; (AA) AA World Travel Library.

1 B Römmelt/Munich Tourist Office; 2-18t AA/T Souter; 4tl C L Schmitt/Munich Tourist Office; 5 R Sterflinger/Munich Tourist Office; 6cl AA/C Sawyer; 6c AA/T Souter; 6cr L Kaster/Munich Tourist Office; 6bl R Hetz/Munich Tourist Office; 6bc AA/T Souter; 6br BBMC Tobias Ranzinger; 7cl AA/M Jourdan; 7c AA/M Jourdan; 7cr AA/M Jourdan; 7bl J Wildgruber/Munich Tourist Office; 7bc AA/M Jourdan; 7br Photodisc; 10tr AA/T Souter; 10/11c B Römmelt/Munich Tourist Office; 10/11b AA/C Sawyer; 11tl AA/M Jourdan; 13tl C Reiter/Munich Tourist Office; 13cl AA/T Souter; 13bl AA/T Souter; 14tr AA/M Jourdan; 14cr AA/C Sawyer; 14bcr Bavaria Tourism; 14br AA/M Jourdan; 16tr C Reiter/ Munich Tourist Office; 16tcr Bavaria Filmstadt; 16cr AA/J Holmes; 16br AA/M Jourdan; 17tl Digitalvision; 17tcl BBMC Tobias Ranzinger; 17cl AA/M Jourdan; 17bl B Römmelt/Munich Tourist Office; 18tr AA/C Sawyer; 18tcr AA/T Souter; 18cr Royalty Free Photodisc; 18br A Müller/Munich Tourist Office; 19tl AA/C Sawyer; 19tcl U Romeis/Munich Tourist Office; 19cl H Schmied/Munich Tourist Office; 19bcl H Gebhardt/Munich Tourist Office; 19bl AA/T Souter; 20/21 C Reiter/Munich Tourist Office; 24l AA/M Jourdan; 24tr T Krüger/Munich Tourist Office; 24br AA/M Jourdan; 25t AA/M Jourdan; 25bl AA/C Sawyer; 25br AA/C Sawyer; 26tl AA/T Souter; 26tr AA/T Souter; 27tl A Müller/Munich Tourist Office; 27c AA/C Sawyer; 27tr A Müller/Munich Tourist Office; 28l H Gebhardt/Munich Tourist Office; 28/29t A Müller/Munich Tourist Office; 28/29b B Römmelt/Munich Tourist Office; 28bc S Böttcher/Munich Tourist Office; 29t H Gebhardt/Munich Tourist Office; 29br F Witzig/Munich Tourist Office; 29bc B Römmelt/Munich Tourist Office; 30tl AA/T Souter; 30tr AA/T Souter; 31tl A Müller/Munich Tourist Office; 31tr A Müller/Munich Tourist Office; 32tl Pat Behnke/Alamy; 32tc AA/T Souter; 32tr AA/T Souter; 33tl B Römmelt/Munich Tourist Office; 33tr C Reiter/Munich Tourist Office; 34-35t AA/M Jourdan; 34bl AA/C Sawyer; 34br C Reiter/Munich Tourist Office; 35 A Müller/Munich Tourist Office; 36 T Krieger/Munich Tourist Office; 37t AA/T Souter; 38t Photodisc; 39t AA/C Sawyer; 40t Digitalvision; 41t AA/M Jourdan; 42t AA/C Sawyer; 43 J Wildgruber/Munich Tourist Office; 46tl Bayerisches Nationalmuseum; 46tc Bayerisches Nationalmuseum; 46tr Bayerisches Nationalmuseum; 47tl AA/T Souter; 47tr BBMC Tobias Ranzinger; 48tl W Hösl/Munich Tourist Office; 48tr U Romeis/Munich Tourist Office; 49tl B Römmelt/Munich Tourist Office; 49tr C Reiter/Munich Tourist Office; 50l W Hösl/Munich Tourist Office; 50tr AA/T Souter; 50br F Mader/Munich Tourist Office; 51t J Lutz/Munich Tourist Office; 51cl AA/T Souter; 51cr AA/M Jourdan; 52-53t AA/M Jourdan; 52bl W Hösl/Munich Tourist Office; 52br AA/C Sawyer; 53b T Krüger/Munich Tourist Office; 54t AA/T Souter; 55t AA/M Chaplow; 56t Photodisc; 57t W Hösl/ Munich Tourist Office; 58t AA/C Sawyer; 59 J Wildgruber/Munich Tourist Office; 62 B Geiges/Munich Tourist Office; 63tl W Hösl/Munich Tourist Office; 63tr AA/C Sawyer; 64l P Scarlandis/Munich Tourist Office; 64tr H Schmied/Munich Tourist Office; 64c AA/M Jourdan; 65t M Prugger/Munich Tourist Office; 65cl AA/T Souter; 65cr AA/M Jourdan; 66t U Romeis/Munich Tourist Office; 66cl AA/T Souter; 66cr A Müller/Munich Tourist Office; 67tl J Wildgruber/Munich Tourist Office; 67cl AA/T Souter; 67r AA/T Souter; 68tl C L Schmitt/Munich Tourist Office; 68tr AA/C Sawyer; 69tl J Sauer/Munich Tourist Office; 69tr J Sauer/Munich Tourist Office; 70l G Blank/Munich Tourist Office; 70tr B Römmelt/ Munich Tourist Office; 70cr AA/M Jourdan; 71t G Blank/Munich Tourist Office; 71cl AA/M Jourdan; 71cr AA/M Jourdan; 72t AA/M Jourdan; 72bl C Reiter/Munich Tourist Office; 72br AA/C Sawyer; 73 AA/T Souter; 74t Photodisc; 75 AA/T Souter; 76t Brand X Pics; 77t AA/M Jourdan; 78 AA/M Jourdan; 79 H Gebhardt/Munich Tourist Office; 82l J Wildgruber/Munich Tourist Office; 82tr P Ruggiero/ Munich Tourist Office; 82cr Olympiapark München; 83t H Gebhardt/Munich Tourist Office; 83c Olympiapark München; 84tl AA/M Jourdan; 84tr B Römmelt/Munich Tourist Office; 84cl AA/M Jourdan; 84cr AA/C Sawyer; 85 C Reiter/Munich Tourist Office; 86tl BMW Pictures; 86tr BMW Pictures; 87-88t AA/M Jourdan; 87bl B Römmelt/Munich Tourist Office; 87br B Römmelt/Munich Tourist Office; 88bl AA/T Souter; 88br R Hetz/Munich Tourist Office; 89t AA/T Souter; 90t AA/T Souter; 91t AA/T Souter; 92t AA/M Jourdan; 93 Bavaria Tourism; 96l Bavaria Filmstadt; 96tr Bavaria Filmstadt; 96cr Bavaria Filmstadt; 97t Bavaria Filmstadt; 97cl Bavaria Filmstadt; 97cr Bavaria Filmstadt; 98l Bavaria Tourism; 98/99t Bavaria Tourism; 98cl Bavaria Tourism; 98c Bavaria Tourism; 98/99 Bavaria Tourism; 99 Bavaria Tourism; 100tl AA/T Souter; 100tr J Wildgruber/Munich Tourist Office; 101-102t AA/M Jourdan; 101bl Allianz Arena; 101br AA/A Baker; 102b imagebroker/Alamy; 103-106t Bavaria Tourism; 103b AA/A Baker; 103c AA/T Souter; 103r Bavaria Tourism; 104 AA/A Baker; 105bl Bavaria Tourism; 105bc AA/T Souter; 105br Bavaria Tourism; 106bl AA/T Souter; 106br AA/T Souter; 107 AA/M Jourdan; 108-112t AA/C Sawyer; 108tr Royalty Free Photodisc; 108cr Stockbyte Royalty Free; 108bcr AA/M Jourdan; 108br AA/M Jourdan; 113 AA/T Souter; 114-125t J Sauer/Munich Tourist Office; 117b AA/T Souter; 120b European Central Bank; 122 AA/T Souter; 124bl AA/C Sawyer; 124bc AA/T Souter; 124br AA/T Souter; 125bl AA/T Souter; 125br AA/C Sawyer

Every effort has been made to trace the copyright holders, and we apologize in advance for any accidental errors. We would be happy to apply the corrections in the following edition of this publication.